T

ANNALS OF A VALLEY

BY ELSIE MURRAY

TIOGA POINT VALLEY LOOKING NORTH

From Painting by Montalant, 1856

WENNAWOODS PUBLISHING
Lewisburg, Pennsylvania
1999

Originally published, Athens, PA (1939)
Reprinted, Lewisburg, PA (1999)

Please direct all correspondence and book orders to:

WENNAWOODS PUBLISHING
RR2 Box 529C Goodman Rd.
Lewisburg, Pennsylvania 17837
800-796-1702

Library of Congress Catalog Card Number 99-61174
ISBN# 1-889037-18-4

****

ACKNOWLEDGMENT

Part I of the *Annals* is a condensed version of certain sections of L. W. Murray's well-documented *Old Tioga Point and Early Athens*, 1908, 666 pages (O.T.P. in the footnotes); checked against her sources and a number of more recent commentaries. Grateful acknowledgment is made also to many descendants of the early settlers of the valley for supplementary information and encouragement.

OTHER BOOKS PUBLISHED BY WENNAWOODS PUBLISHING

The Indian Chiefs of Pennsylvania (1927)
By C.Hale Sipe

The Indian Wars of Pennsylvania (1931)
By C.Hale Sipe

A History of the Indian Villages & Place Names of Pennsylvania (1928)
By Dr. George P. Donehoo

The Wilderness Trail, Volumes 1&2 (1911)
By Charles A. Hanna

Early History of Western Pennsylvania (1846)
By I. D. Rupp

Conrad Weiser, Friend of Colonist & Mohawk (1945)
By Paul A. W. Wallace

Loudon's Indian Narratives (1888)
By Archibald Loudon

The History of an Expedition Against Fort DuQuesne in 1755 (1856)
By Winthrop Sargent

Early Western Journals (1904)
By Reuben Gold Thwaites

Thirty Thousand Miles With John Heckewelder (1958)
By Paul A. W. Wallace

A Pennsylvania Bison Hunt (1915)
By Henry W. Shoemaker

Luke Swetland's Captivity (1915)
By Edward Merrifield

David Zeisberger's History of the Northern American Indians in 18th Century Ohio, New York & Pennsylvania (1910)
Edited by Archer Butler Hulbert and William Nathaniel Schwarze

The Lenape and Their Legends (1885)
By Daniel G. Brinton, A.M., M.D

Journals of Samuel Maclay While Surveying the West Branch of the Susquehanna, the Sinnemahoning and the Allegheny Rivers in 1790 (1887)
Edited by John F. Meginness

PART ONE

PROLOGUE: VALLEY PANORAMA

The stranger driving north from Towanda[1] toward the New York-Pennsylvania border faces a tempting choice of routes, both picturesque. The less frequented crosses the Susquehanna by the long Sheshequin bridge, and following the east bank of the river climbs the Narrows by a roadway narrow and perilous until recent years. Presently, at the old Turn o' Rocks, a vista opens through the hemlocks, worth even in horse-and-buggy days the risk of collision with a passing vehicle. For the cliff drops sheer 150 feet to the river, and a green valley floor shot with reaches of silvery water stretches north from the hill's base into the misty distance. *Old Tioga Point*—gateway to the Empire State to the north, the natural link between the central Pennsylvania coalfields and the Finger Lakes with their vineyards and orchards, their salt and gypsum—lies at your feet—a gigantic green 'Arrow' pointing south.

A strategic spot since the first human foot trod its trails, the Valley has served as campsite and highway for Indian, trader, adventurer, soldier, emigrant, and tourist toward Niagara in turn. Populous villages of Andaste warriors clustered here, their watchfires smouldering on the western heights, in the days when Samuel Champlain and Captain John Smith were adventuring abroad. In 1779, a third of the Continental army encamped below, 5000 strong, waiting impatiently for General Sullivan to lead them against the Iroquois and Tory. In 1786, General Ethan Allen and his Green Mountain Boys were summoned here to insert a fourteenth state between the upper and the nether millstones—New York and Pennsylvania. In 1859, this was a famous stage-coach stop for picturesque west-bound travellers—Frémont, Greeley, Giddings. Canal boats discharged their cargoes below near the headquarters of the new North Branch Canal, and a packet built at West Athens, aptly named the *Gazelle*, plied to and fro to Towanda.

Yet for all its weight of old tradition, Indian, military, economic, the little valley, known in old surveys as the 'Indian Arrow,' contains within its limits a scant ten square miles. Roughly triangular in contour, like the famous forks of the Delaware, its base is defined by the misty Waverly hills to the north, just over the State line, with the golf-links and Iron Kettle Inn on their southern slopes. Its apex is the meeting of the Chemung and Susquehanna at our feet—Teaoga, in the Indian vernacular, the meeting of the trails. The heavily wooded hill walls of the two rivers—the looming leonine bulk of Round Top on the west, Prospect and Orange Hills and their tapering northern ridges on the east, their topmost soil burned red with old Indian watchfires, enclose its sides.

[1] On the Sullivan Trail, Route 309, Bradford County, Pennsylvania.

Etched on the landscape's face traces of a million years of geologic time, ten centuries of aboriginal occupation, and a century and a half of white man's endeavor, are visible from the vantage point of the 'Turn.' The slow work of frost and sun, air, ice and water have lowered the once lofty peaks, and scoured away their coal or gold-bearing strata. Towering snowdrifts and a mighty tongue of glacial ice more than once have filled the valley, grinding the cliffs sheer now on the east, now on the west. Three levels of river terraces mark the successive heights of floods released by the melting of this titanic ice-field, whose waters are said once to have flowed north into the Great Lakes and the St. Lawrence.

Unlike the Lehigh running swift in its narrow gorge, the Susquehanna twists its serpentine way over an old flood-plain of fragments scoured by moving ice from New York, Canadian and perhaps New England bedrock. A flat-topped mass of glacial rubbish or moraine, known locally as Spanish Hill, rises like a huge inverted scalloped caketin 230 feet above the valley floor to the north and west. The rock strata exposed by glacial cuts along the hillsides, lying one above another like the leaves of a book, are shales of the Devonian period, full of the brachiopods, spirifers, and broken crinoid stems of an ancient seashore.* * * So much for the geological preface to Amerindian and white occupation.

The aboriginal history of the valley turns on its topography. The tributaries of the Chemung and Susquehanna[2] command wide reaches of New York State, west and east. Southward, a network of creeks connects the North with the West Branch, hence with the western approach to Pennsylvania. This brought converging streams of aboriginal emigration from all quarters of the compass to Teaoga, the 'meeting of the waters.' Here lay the junction of all trails—Algonkin, Andaste, Iroquois in turn. A closer view would disclose the midden-heaps of river mussel shells, the ancient pottery and flint factory sites on the Point and the east shore; the rows of fire-pits and old buried corn caches, or the cairn of boulders marking an ancient burial location in the 'Neck.' At this height, however, only the wide reaches of Indian cornfields and grazing grounds along the river catch the eye, notably the five-mile stretch of Esther's Flats, and the 'Point' of the great notched 'Arrowhead' outlined by the approach, divergence and final union of the rivers—camping-place in turn of many migrants. The flat ten-acre top of Spanish Hill is lost in the northern perspective.

The century and a half of civilized enterprise is etched more clearly on the panorama. Even Montalant's painting of 1856 reveals the ruthless lumbering of the hillsides—preface to the great flood of '65. Scattered farmhouses, a couple of bridges, clustering roofs and spires at the 'Neck' define early Athens, old Tioga Point. A tiny haze of buildings on the northeast at the point where Shepard Creek emerges from the hills indicates Milltown, the nucleus of Sayre, and a mere pine-dotted plain the area where the modern railroad town has since expanded. A faint fringe of houses along the east-west road connecting the Owego and Newtown routes forecasts

[2] *Chemung* is said to be the Indian word for *horn*, derived from the huge mammoth tusks excavated along the rivers. *Susquehanna* is variously defined as *winding, rily, river of many islets*.

Waverly. This was all that registered in the eye of the itinerant French painter who raised his easel in the mid-century on Prospect.

Today, from the Chemung bridge at Athens to the Waverly hills, a massed array of roofs and treetops testifies to the growth and coalescence of the three villages, most rapid in the last sixty years. Rotarians' signs along the highway alone define the transition from Sayre to Athens, a short stretch of open fields only separates South Waverly from Sayre. Towering smokestacks disclose the location of the Robert Packer Hospital and Guthrie Clinic, the pride of Northern Pennsylvania; the Ingersoll-Rand Pneumatic Tool Works, near the old Union Bridge Company site; the Lehigh Valley yards and shops at Sayre (named for an early official of the railroad); the Knitting Mills on the site of the old Ovenshire farm. Glittering lines of rails running north and south along the river or east and west at the triangle's base define the routes of the Lehigh Valley, the Erie, and the Delaware, Lackawanna and Western; a half dozen bridges and viaducts, and gleaming ribbons of concrete or asphalt, the modern highways. Scattered over the prospect rise a multitude of church spires. Like a gigantic dragon-fly a mailplane courses high over the valley.

A closer view would reveal the destruction of Indian sites by railway cuts or the undermining of floods, the ravages and altered courses of creeks that once turned scores of mill-wheels and supplied pioneers with planks and flour. Their old forest cover in the hills destroyed, in midsummer Franklin, Satterlee, Shepard, Tutelo, Ganestoga (Dry Brook), Murray and Wolcott[3] creeks are mere dry beds of boulders, white as bleached bones, except for infrequent cloudbursts. The old location at the mouth of Murray's creek where 60-foot lumbermen's 'arks' were once launched has expanded, however, to a village—Greene's Landing, now dairy country.[4]

From the dusky hemlocks overhead, where recent road work has blasted away the last remnants of the Great Warrior Path, come the staccato phrases of a warbler of cool northern woods, the black-throated green. Below, where motionless fishermen in flat-bottomed boats replace swift-moving Indian canoemen, an occasional osprey competes with belted kingfishers and bitterns for minnows or young bass. Swallow-like, patterned sandpipers skim the shallows, shepherding their young among the sedges along the Point with sharp 'peet, peet.' White-barked sycamores line the shores and afford shelter for the grazing herds.

How many citizens of the plain below, one wonders, know that one of the most famous, indeed the last surviving signer of the Declaration of Independence, at his death head of the Baltimore and Ohio and the wealthiest man in the States, in 1806 held title to many acres in the 'Arrow,' planning to make the Susquehanna the main route to the West?[5] Once the head of

[3] Named for a local Paul Bunyan who once hitched twenty span of oxen to a log-cabin and drove it to a political campaign meeting as a mascot.

[4] Over at the foot of Round Top, old *Stoneport* where the Stones built and launched boats for canal and river traffic, until the flood of '65 washed away shipyard and contents, a cluster of colored lights at night betrays the last word in modernity—a group of tourist cabins.

[5] Charles Carroll of Carrollton. Two other signers equally famous—Robert and Gouverneur Morris—once owned extensive tracts just to the east and south. Timothy Pickering, Revolutionary Quartermaster, Postmaster and Secretary of War and State in Washington's cabinet, was one of the first patentees of the site of Sayre.

navigation of the river, a node in the natural trade route between the Chesapeake and the Great Lakes, the Wyoming coal-fields and the Erie Canal; at the outset of our era of expansion, on the line of migration to the newly opened New York State lands, our Valley played no small rôle in the evolution of greater America. In its annals figure men of nation-wide repute. Some of these *dramatis personae* occupied themselves with its destiny from a distance—General George Washington and Benjamin Franklin; or were summoned by opposing parties to its assistance—Ethan Allen and Timothy Pickering. Following the precedent set by the Indian chieftains Teedyuskung and Brant, General John Sullivan made it a military rendezvous. Others halted here on the trail to record their impressions, among them Conrad Weiser, sturdy Palatinate and Indian interpreter; St. John Crèvecoeur, the 'American Farmer'; the genial Quaker botanist, John Bartram; and Alexander Wilson, poet-ornithologist and neighbor of Robert Burns, scoffing at our delay in finishing our schoolhouse "while taverns rise on every side." Later came the duke de La Rochefoucauld-Liancourt, exiled French statesman and reformer, comparing these same taverns a trifle superciliously with those of Paris. A goodly number, offshoots of the early American stock that gave us colonial governors, Revolutionary generals, West Indian merchants and sea-captains, transplanted their families here, after the successive depressions of the Revolutionary War and that of 1812. These sturdy colonists cleared and cultivated the soil, built roads and bridges, mills and homesteads, and developed the Valley as a vital link in the great continental system of canals and railroads and commerce of our Republic.

The racial stock of the original settlers was varied. Scotch-Irish, Welsh, English, Holland-Dutch and Palatinate-German ('Pennsylvania Dutch') settlers felled the great pine forests, and staked out their claims below. The majority came direct from Connecticut, or by way of Wyoming, 'old Ulster' or other Susquehannah Company townships, and were men of independent character, enterprise, education and ideals, who had done their bit in the Revolutionary army. Some, discouraged by the snarl of overlapping Pennsylvania and Connecticut land claims, or eager for new frontiers to conquer, passed on shortly to become the pioneers of westerly and southern states—New York, Ohio, Illinois, Michigan, Oregon, California, Carolina. The Alexanders, town builders, with the future father-in-law of Thomas Edison among them; the Paines, travellers and tree-lovers, men of culture and public spirit; the Shipmans, promotors of early foundries and industries, builders of Clovercroft; the Saltmarshes, a post-route, stage-and-tavern family; and certain Morley, Shepard, Tozer, Spalding and Murray descendants, joined this tide of emigrants. Quaint slabs in the old burying-grounds record their passage.

Others remained to place their mark on the Valley in the guise of dignified homesteads or public institutions; to give their names to the creeks they had used for water-power, or the streets where formerly stood their homes or shops. Prominent among these were the Shepards, Herricks, Hopkins, Satterlees, Franklins, Spaldings, McDuffees, Hustons, Harrises, Paines, Morleys, Tozers, Welles, Murrays and Westbrooks. The younger sons of many whose early enterprise guided the industrial growth of the valley, and established roads, bridges, schools, newspapers, and churches, preferring urban to rural life, went to swell the ranks of bankers, financiers and scholars in the cities of Elmira, Wilkes Barre, Brooklyn, New York and Chicago. Meanwhile, with the coming of canal, railroad and shops there has been a continual influx of new blood, Irish, Italian and Ukrainian.

Stronghold of the Carantouannais in the early 17th century; in the 18th the southern gateway of the Iroquois, and site of Sullivan's basal fort, our Valley became in pioneer days the focus of Connecticut-Pennsylvania land-feuds. Head of navigation on the Susquehanna, and a famous stage-stop in the early half of the 19th century, in the second half it functioned as headquarters for the hundred-mile stretch of North Branch Canal that tied the Wyoming coal-fields to the Finger Lake region and the West. Home of the projector of the New York and Pennsylvania Canal and Railroad Company, C. F. Welles, Jr., of Athens, who built the railroad on the abandoned tow-path, it was later the residence of Robert Packer,[6] superintendent, then president of the N. Y. and Pa. Railroad which finally amalgamated with the Lehigh Valley. From 1814 to 1870 seat of the widely known Athens Academy, with its long roll of distinguished graduates; site also of a remarkably varied succession of industries, including the Union Bridge Works, the Teaoga Valley obviously merits more detailed study than a mere panoramic view affords. Descending from the heights, let us trace its history briefly in the light of documents gathered by a long line of scholars and antiquarians, and stored in the Tioga Point Museum.[7]

Our survey will touch in turn upon the *aboriginal inhabitants of the Valley*; *Sullivan's sojourn here in 1779* on the way to Newtown and Genesee Castle; *the pioneer settlers of 1786 and Pennsylvania-Connecticut land feuds*; running swiftly over *the evolution of transportation* in the first part of the 19th century, from stage-route and canal to railroad; the succeeding *diversification of industry*, and cultural development; and the final *transformation of the twentieth century*—era of electricity, automobile and radio.

[6] Son of Asa, projector of the lower sections of the Lehigh Valley Railroad from Mauch Chunk to Easton.

[7] Founded in 1897 by the descendants of early settlers.

I. OUR INDIAN PREDECESSORS IN THE VALLEY

Whoever has rambled along our rivers as a boy, filling his pockets with exquisitely chipped arrowheads or the many-patterned potsherds of Esther's Flats, must have puzzled over the identity of the primitive hunters and housewives who (lacking metal and machinery) fashioned weapons from flint and cooking-vessels from clay. Additional problems confront the student, glancing back through history.

Who were our forerunners in the Valley, leaving us a legacy of liquid-syllabled Indian names—Susquehanna, Wappasenink, Wilawana; trails running east and north and south; corn-fields along the rivers, and unscarred forests? Legends survive of a few spectacular chieftains of historic times—Shikellimy, the wise Oneida; Teedyuscung, the "aboriginal Falstaff" of the Delawares; Esther Montour, the enigmatical French-Indian Queen—all of whom lived or camped or traded at Teaoga.

But what of the tribes native here in the days of gold-seeking Spaniards and the fabled last stand of De Soto's followers on Spanish Hill? In the year of Captain John Smith's rendezvous at the Susquehanna's mouth with giantlike "Werowances," clad in skins of bear and wolf, who paddled down the river to greet him? Curiosity piques us also as to the warriors whose aid young Brulé, Champlain's scout, sought here in 1615. And who were the native trappers and hunters holding title to this area in 1682 when William Penn followed the fur-trading Swedes up the Delaware?

No sooner are these riddles solved than others rise to vex us. Who were the kindly hosts who fed and lodged the Moravian peace-makers of the early 18th century on their toilsome passage through Teaoga? Who knows the clan and totem of the villagers ousted by Hartley and Sullivan from the valley in 1778-79? And what lingering groups, copper-skinned, black-haired, aquiline-nosed, guarding the graves of their ancestors, did the pioneers of 1786 find cabined here, to borrow skins and corn and mortars of, in exchange for guns and powder? History surely has preserved the roster of the tribes who gathered in a last rally at Teaoga in 1790-91, to exchange broadsides of rhetoric with the land commissioners, Thomas Morris and Timothy Pickering, and maneuvre for a last grip on their lands in the Empire State?

On many of these matters we must admit dense ignorance. Knowledge of our immediate predecessors in the Valley is a patchwork of surmise from old maps, travellers' journals, stray entries in colonial archives and treaties, pieced together with deductions from excavated aboriginal sites. Yet without this patchwork knowledge the early period of white occupation would remain a riddle. We would lack the key to concentration here in 1779 of an army of 5000 Continentals under Sullivan. The early pioneer decades, with Yankee arrayed against Pennamite, and Col. John Franklin held in jail for treason, would prove equally perplexing.

Fragmentary and circuitous though it is, the evidence is worth assembling. It connects us with the four chief colonial ventures of the early 17th century: with New Sweden whose colonists bought furs of our Indians (whom they called Minquas); with Jamestown, whose hero, Captain John Smith, eulogized our Susquehannocks as fine specimens of manhood; with Quebec, whose founder, Champlain, sent here for military aid; with New Amsterdam, whose launching by Holland traders was inspired by reports made by three Dutchman held captive by our local Indians, no less than by the voyage of the Half Moon on the Hudson.[1]

Teaoga a Natural Key Site

Many circumstances conspired to put Teaoga (*Meeting of the Waters of the Chemung and Susquehanna*) on the page of history. Not the least of these was its strategic site, as a glance at the map reveals. The tributaries of the Chemung—the Cohocton, Canisteo and Tioga—lead by short portages to the headwaters of the western Finger Lakes, and of the Genesee and Allegheny rivers—hence to the Great Lakes and the Ohio. The upper confluents of the Susquehanna—the Cayuta, Tioughnioga, Chenango, Unadilla and Otsego segments—interweave with the sources of the eastern Finger Lakes, with Mohawk and Delaware headwaters also. Only a short

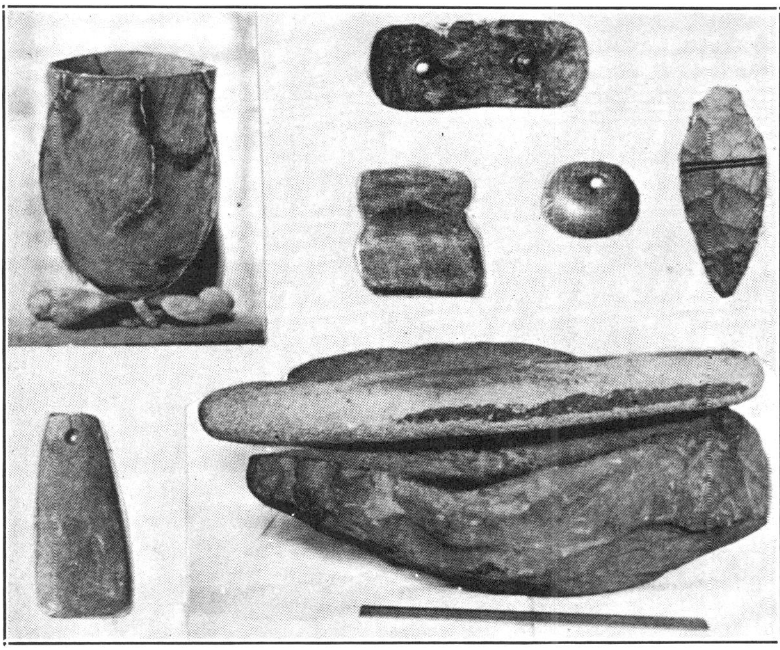

EQUIPMENT OF AN ALGONKIN FAMILY
Food-Mortar and Pestle. Cooking-Pot. Spear-Head, Canoe Anchor, Amulets

journey below the Point, the Oscohu (Sugar Creek) and the Tawandae (Towanda Creek) lead down toward the West Branch of the Susquehanna (by the Sheshequin Path). The great hunting-grounds of the plateaux above Wyoming, jasper and quartzite quarries, and the fisheries of the Chesapeake, lay on the direct course south. Here was the natural forking of the trails—the Great Warrior and Minnisink Paths.

Algonkin Fisher and Andaste Town Builder

The earliest aboriginal arrival after the melting of the glacier has left us no certain evidence of his identity. It seems probable, however, that he

[1] The three Dutchmen who furnished facts for the Figurative Map are believed to have been held at Ogehage (Sugar Creek). See O.T.P., 31-32.

was a primitive *Algonkin* fisherman and hunter, of remote Asiatic ancestry, who had made his way gradually across Canada from Behring Straits, with his stone net-sinkers, his stemmed darts or spearheads, his birchbark or steatite cooking vessels. With him he may have brought as well his polished whale-tail ceremonials, his carved totem amulets, and a host of magical rites and superstitions engendered in the land of the Midnight Sun.[2] Roughly speaking, he was on the same cultural level as our cave-dwelling Old Stone Age ancestor of Europe, though lacking the latter's skill as draughtsman and artist.

Approaching along one of the many waterways, he and his later kinsmen have left ample evidence of their grasp of Teaoga's practical resources, whether or not they foresaw its strategic value. A great river up which shad and eels made their way freely from salt water; creeks full of mussels and fish, the osiers and flat stones of which furnished material for nets and sinkers; and boulders readily shaped into mortars for grinding nuts and acorns. Here were also maple groves which would provide sugar even in years of famine, heavily wooded hills to which to retreat in flood-time, and abundant game. Very crude grooved axes and pestles found at the foot of Spanish Hill and at Sheshequin suggest this early migrant may have arrived with little skill or patience in tool-making, though sinker-stones for nets and rough spearheads are abundant.

The second wave of Algonkin migration had probably acquired rude pottery-making,[3] corn culture, and use of bow and arrow from Iroquoian contacts. The remnant of De Soto's followers who are conjectured to have pushed their way up the Ohio and down the tributaries of the Susquehanna, to give Spanish Hill its name, may have found here descendants of this second Algonkin infiltration. It appears to have spread fanwise over Canada and down into the northern regions of our territory.[4] The Indians encountered by the early colonists of Virginia and New England, Powhatans, Narragansetts, Pequots, Mohegans, all belonged linguistically to this group; as did the Lenni Lenape or Delaware, the Nanticoke and Shawanese, forced later into our area by white aggression.

Later than the early Algonkin, but long before Europe had turned envious eyes on the gold and copper ornaments of the aborigine, his game and peltries, his corn and squash fields, warlike bands speaking an Iroquoian dialect, and best known as *Andastes*, made their way up the Mississippi and the Ohio and down the tributaries of the Susquehanna. Certain clues connect them with the mysterious Mound Builders of the Mississippi watershed. In any case, their long trek across the continent appears to have led down the west coast from Behring Straits to the Basket-Maker (later Pueblo) settlements on the mesas of the Southwest, where they may have acquired pottery-making and corn culture from Mayan sources; thence to the Mississippi basin.

---

[2] Sometimes classified as Pre-Algonkin, and linked with the Beothuk or Red Paint People of Newfoundland and Maine: a group whose igloo-shaped huts, semi-lunar knives and other artifacts ally them with the Eskimo. See C. C. Willoughby, *Antiquities of the New England Indians*, 1935, 60 f. There may, of course, have been earlier waves of migration, separated by centuries from the Algonkin infiltration, parallel with the Yuma and Folsom cultures, traces of which have recently been discovered on the east slope of he Rockies. Folsom-like points are found in our vicinity.

[3] Crude, thick, pebble-tempered, badly shaped and roughly decorated with corncob, fabric or punchwork. Along the east bank of the Susquehanna from Sheshequin to the State Line are almost continuous signs of Algonkin occupation.

[4] For what purports to be the Delaware's own tradition of this migration, the Walum Olum, see D. G. Brinton, *The Lenape and Their Legends*, 1885.

At Teaoga, they found fertile river terraces, enriched by annual floods, on which to plant their corn and squash; quail in the valleys, deer and elk in the hills, bear, wolf and beaver for peltry. Here also, though the bed-rock is shale, were a variety of glacier-quarried stones from which to shape their tools—granite for mullers, greenstone and flint nodules for celts and triangular arrowpoints; with beds of clay to tempt their potters to new artistry. Hemlock, elm and birch provided bark for their curved roof-tree lodges and canoes; balsam, straight poles for palisaded walls, to repel wild beasts and strangers. Round Top, Spanish Hill and Turn o' Rocks offered craggy lookouts over the rivers, from which to sight approaching foes. The soil on the southern lookout of Spanish Hill is burned red to a depth of several feet with centuries of watch-fires.

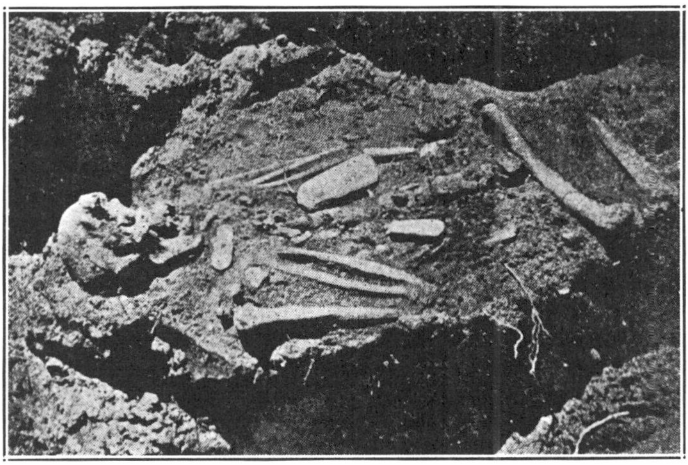

Andaste Burial at Athens
Flexed Skeleton of Chief, with his Possessions. Found under Cairn of Stones 1883-96.

Possible Contacts with Jamestown and Quebec: Carantouan. Populous villages, whose burial places yield rare finds, were scattered through the valley.[5] Not improbably they despatched a delegation down to the Chesapeake in 1608 to impress Captain John Smith, hero of Jamestown, with their prowess and stature, and draw his imprecations on the rocks that barred progress upriver to inspect their villages.[6] Among these visitors may have been the chieftain exhumed in 1895 from an old orchard on South Main Street, Athens, buried with the high honors of a stone-slab coffin, a mighty food-jar, celt, stone tomahawk and arrows, a cairn of boulders to mark the spot, and a circle of his clansmen around him. He is believed to be Andaste, distant kinsman of the Seneca, Cayuga and Mohawk of the Iroquois Confederacy to the north, but their sworn enemy. A rare jar with

[5] Unlike the early nomadic Algonkin, the Andaste—a name sometimes translated as 'town-dweller'—lived in community lodges, long dwellings accommodating several families, with individual alcoves along the sides, and individual firepits down the center —in short, an early form of apartment house. A group of these was surrounded by a palisade. The name Andaste was given them by the Jesuit Fathers of Canada.

[6] Smith called them Sasquesahanoughs, after the river. For further facts on this group, see A. B. Skinner, *The Andaste*, in *Susquehanna River Expedition of 1916*, 1938, 44-67; and D. A. Cadzow, *Susquehannock Indians*, 1936, 15-38.

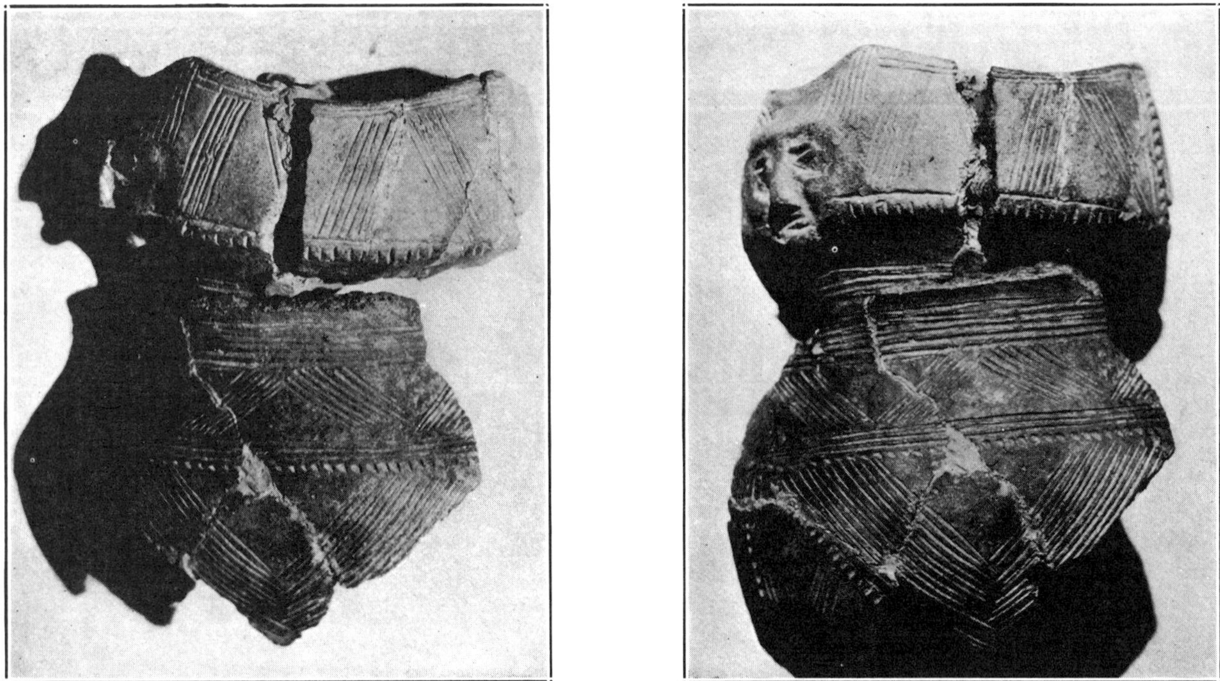

Andaste Portrait Jar
Faces of Chieftain and Wife, or of Good and Evil Spirits, with Chevron Pattern

faces modelled in low relief, conjectured to represent the Good and Evil Spirits, was unearthed in the same cemetery—but no trade articles, unless the fragmentary blue beads found came from Smith's Virginia glass factory.

Fame of these villages, once able to furnish a quota of 800 warriors, spread even to Canada and reached the ears of Samuel de Champlain. For in 1615, while aiding his Huron allies to assault an Iroquois fort near Lake Oneida, the founder of Quebec sent his young scout Brulé with Huron escorts to beg help from the Carantouannais, located by connoisseurs near our Spanish Hill. Unluckily for Champlain, the reinforcements arrived too late, the Huron war party had retired to Canada, with their wounded leader in a litter. Luckily for Brulé, however, who returned to winter in our valley, becoming the next spring the first European navigator and explorer to its mouth of the Susquehanna. A low stone monument on Spanish Hill marks the supposed spot of his encounter with the Carantouannais, and of the subsequent martial revels which delayed departure northward.

The Hill, a curious glacial moraine formation of sand, cobblestone and boulders in South Waverly (northwest of Athens) rises to a height of 230 feet above the valley, commanding fine views north and south, up the Chemung and down the Susquehanna. Since 1878, when General John S. Clark, an old scouting officer of the Civil War, identified it with the aid of Champlain's Journal and map as Brulé's rendezvous it has been known as *Carantouan,* a name variously interpreted as meaning *great tree,* or *great horn.* Balsam fir is believed to have grown on the hill, possibly in the marshy sink-holes at the rear. Mammoth tusks have been exhumed from the banks of the nearby Chemung, giving the river its Indian name Conongue. We leave the choice of interpretations of Carantouan to the reader.

In 1933-5, Ellsworth C. Cowles, archaeologist for Tioga Point Museum, uncovered post holes of a quadrangular palisaded Indian village[7] at the foot of the hill, with a ceremonial hearth of animal contour just outside, used perhaps in some magical hunting ceremony, to the accompaniment of weird music. A typical short Andaste smoking pipe, a food jar with incised chevron collar and a copper bead were exhumed in a nearby burial. These and other recent findings in pottery and chipped flint match those both of the Andaste burial plot at Athens and of Susquehannock sites far down the river. *Carantouannais* was apparently Champlain's name for an Iroquoian group identical with the Andaste of the Jesuit missionaries, and kinsmen of the Susquehannock of the lower valley—Captain John Smith's Sasquesahanoughs.

As for Brulé, a name earned by two miraculous escapes from the stake, he suffered ultimately a fate which renders futile our petitioning Canada for his bones. Like Weiser, he had lived with the Indians as a boy, learning their dialect—and in nine cases out of ten was their match in strategy. The tenth case proved his undoing. In revenge for some alleged treachery, he was killed by his Indian allies and piously devoured, in the belief that his prowess would be thus magically acquired by his captors.

Up to the close of the 17th century the Susquehanna was an Indian river, defended valiantly by the Andaste against fierce assaults of their blood-brothers the 'Sinnikers' (Senecas) and 'Caiuckers' (Cayugas). The "Relations" of the Jesuit Fathers (French missionaries among the Canadian

---

[7] Whether Algonkin or Iroquoian remains to be determined by future excavation. Some day, it is hoped, this entire site will become a state or national park, with restoration of the village.

'Spanish Hill'
The Carantouan Stronghold of Champlain's Scout Brulé?

Hurons), Colonial Records, Champlain's and Captain John Smith's maps and accounts of their adventures, and early Swedish historians are our chief sources of information on these manoeuvres, and the Spartan chararacter and escapades of the spirited Andaste boys. Surface and other findings indicate that in the days when unbroken forest covered northern Pennsylvania the Andastes were entrenched on craggy heights at Teaoga, at Fort Hill (near Elmira), at Ogehage (Sugar Creek, near the Oscalui marker), Gahontoto (Wyalusing) and many other nearby points of vantage.

Iroquois Conquest: Subject Tribes Migrate to the Valley

By the time of the arrival of Penn and his co-religionists on the Schuylkill, smallpox, white treachery and the fierce jealousy of their northern kinsmen had virtually exterminated the Andaste on the Susquehanna. The victorious Seneca, Cayuga, Mohawk, Oneida and Onondaga[8] banded themselves together in the formidable *Iroquois Confederacy* (the first United States of America), extending their warlike sway from the St. Lawrence to the James, from the Hudson to the Ohio. Declaring our Teaoga the southern gateway to their 'Long House,' they stationed a Cayuga chieftain here to guard the passage,[9] and supervise the dozen different subject tribes they had colonized along the Susquehanna—Tutelo, Nanticoke, Munsey, Mohegan, Shawnee—all Algonkin except the first, who were of Sioux stock. Shikellimy, an Oneida chief (probably part white), was assigned a similar and more extensive function at Shamokin (Sunbury), where the West Branch joins the North, with instructions to control rum traffic and the reckless bargaining away of Indian hunting-grounds and homes. For the annals of this century in the valley are full of tales of raids and murders, of the inroads of white man's fire-water and diseases, of unfair or broken land-contracts.[10] The folly of admitting the white race to trails and hunting-grounds was at last apparent. "Your horses and cows have eat the grass our deer used to feed on." "The land lasts always but the goods waste soon away." "The justice of the Great White Father across the water is not our justice," the eloquent Indian chieftains protest in sorrow or indignation at the joint council-fires at Lancaster and Bethlehem.

In the first half of the 18th century the victorious Iroquois Confederacy as a matter of fact was under stiff pressure from the English on the east and the French on the west. With La Salle's discovery of the Mississippi the vast province of Louisiana had sprung into being, and fur-traders and fort-builders were soon pushing up the Ohio into western Pennsylvania. Along the Delaware and Hudson, there were fresh bands of settlers, new towns rising. Hemmed in between the two parties of intruders, the little union of 50 Iroquois villages maintained itself through the long wars of Catholic France against Protestant England (1698-1763) by dangling a promise of alliance now before French, now before English emissaries.

Dual Rôle of Teaoga in the Franco-British Colonial Wars. In this century of fierce rivalry for New World land and revenues, of bitter struggle be-

[8] Streets on the northern border of Sayre perpetuate these names. The Tuscarora was a southerly group taken in about 1721, bringing the total to six, hence the *Six Nations*. Hiawatha, Onondaga pacifist, is the fabled originator of the plan for confederation.

[9] Perhaps accompanied by others of his tribe, since a Cayuga village, Ganatockeracht, was reported between Spanish Hill and the Chemung in 1750 by the 29-year-old Moravian bishop, Cammerhof.

[10] Indian culture furnished little analogue of the European concept of land as property and its legal transference.

tween the original owners of the forest and encroaching whites, Teaoga registers as delicately as a seismograph every major colonial event.[11] Delaware resentment at dispossession, Braddock's disaster on the Monongahela, Pontiac's War on the Ohio, Connecticut aggression in the Wyoming Valley, are reflected in the ebb and flow of peace emissaries and war parties along the river, in the long canoe trains of migrants seeking new homes. Indian orchards fall to decay and cornfields lie fallow at the Point, when the Governor of Pennsylvania declares war against the marauding Delaware, drops Penn's peace policy to offer a scalp bounty, and sets the neutral line at the point *where the 'Tioga Branch'* (Chemung) *enters the Susquehanna* (1763). Teaoga becomes a no-man's land, where one passes the night only, en route to Niagara or Onondaga, during Pontiac's War.

Throughout this era, the only guarantee of peace between red race and white lay in the generosity of the latter (a matter of lavish entertainment, of gifts of guns and gold-laced uniforms—and rum), plus a certain measure of mutual understanding. Hardly a dozen individuals—all associated with Teaoga annals—were equipped with a talent for the latter, to the best of our knowledge. These were whites who had known Indian foster-parents, acquiring their tongue and knowledge of their ways, notably the German-born Conrad Weiser, saved from starvation as a lad by a Mohawk chief's hospitality; and Shikellimy, white captive reared by Oneidas to a chieftainship, Christian convert, man of honor and sworn enemy of rum.[12] Captain Newcastle, on the contrary, was an Indian reared in William Penn's household. There was a white strain in the Montours (some say the blood of old Count Frontenac); while Sir William Johnson and Christian Frederick Post had taken Indian mates to dispense the hospitality of their households, and induct them into the subtleties of Indian thought.

As for William Penn's policy of perpetual peace with the Indian, so solemnly inaugurated under a spreading oak, it had lapsed completely with his heirs, as had that of Lord Baltimore with our Susquehannocks earlier. The Moravian Brethren—spiritual heirs of the persecuted John Huss of Bohemia—had taken up Penn's fallen standard, however. For nearly forty years they journeyed up and down the trails of Pennsylvania, on horseback, afoot and by canoe; sustained by the mirage of universal peace hovering ever before them; preaching, baptising, founding missions (tiny centres of civilization) as did the Padres of California. Like the Jesuit Fathers of New France, also, they willingly shared bed and board with their hosts, lean or plenty as might be—thin broth or venison haunch. And often the pleas of a Post or a Zeisberger proved the final pennyweight on the scales, tilting away from war. Every excursion was to them a Pilgrims' Progress, and our landscape from Spanish Hill to Wyalusing, if we but knew it, is set thick with invisible pious guideposts—Haven of Grace, Tents of Peace, Pentacostal Hill—marking their halts. Especially among the imaginative and superstitious Delawares were they successful, though sometimes their doctrines turned against them, and their hosts closed their doors, for 'the corn would no longer grow,' or they had 'cast a spell on the deer.'

The factors making for discord are an old story. The Indian's sense of

---

[11] See Colonial Records, II-III; and Pennsylvania Archives, VII-IX.

[12] Stationed at Shamokin where the North and West Branches meet, the Iroquois viceregent, Shikellimy, built his house on posts, and when the rum kegs were broached, drew up his steps.

justice, his resentment of trickery or broken word, was as keen as a white man's. In the score of the Lenape against the white (and against his Iroquoian masters) specific grievances accumulated. First came the settlement of German migrants from Schoharie north of Penn's purchase line on the Lehigh. There followed the tricky execution of the Walking Purchase on the Delaware with three trained *runners*—one of whom covered 68 miles in the day and a half allotted.[13] Next came the Connecticut intrusion (following the treacherous sale to the Susquehannah Company of the precise tract assigned the Lenape by the Confederacy to replace the forfeited Delaware Valley—the lovely Wyoming); necessitating a second forced move to Teaoga.

Small wonder that the worm (or rather the turtle, Teedyuscung's totem) turned at last, and the peace-loving Lenape threw off the yoke of their overbearing Iroquoian masters. Exchanging pestle for tomahawk, in 1754-5 they rose against the white transgressors (English and German settlers on the Pennsylvania frontier); lifting the hatchet in the cause of France, whose agents, penetrating easily from Fort Niagara, had long been active among them on the Susquehanna.

Grievances of the Lenni Lenape. Early in 1723, there had passed the Point at Teaoga raft on raft of migrating German peasants and their families, land-hungry refugees lured from the starving, war-ridden Palatinate by Queen Anne's promises, from the Mohawk and the Schoharie by the hope of better treatment from Penn's governor. Cattle were driven along the narrow trail through the narrows. Stray fawns, wild duck and pigeons and shad supplemented their meagre fare. Followed presently across the Atlantic by shipload on shipload of fellow refugees, to be known colloquially as the 'Pennsylvania Dutch,' these weary exiles passed up the Tulpehocken to found Reading (later Lancaster and York).[14] Some took up farms in the 'Forks of the Delaware' where Bethlehem and Allentown were to rise, beyond the limits of Penn's land purchases of the Lenni Lenape. This was the beginning of the end of the peace policy of William Penn the Quaker with the Algonkin group he found in possession of the Delaware valley. What followed?

In the hall of the Historical Society of Pennsylvania in Philadelphia hang the dusky fading portraits of two 'Signers' who unlike the famous fifty-five of a half-century later, whose memory is enshrined in Independence Hall, are infamous among their people. These dusky tragic faces are those of Lapowinsae (He-Who-Gets-Provisions) and Tishcohan, Lenni Lenape snared into signing the detested 'Walking Purchase.' For in 1737 Penn's heirs, urged by the Lenape to adjust the disputed boundary, guilefully employed runners instead of walkers in the unfinished three-day jaunt agreed upon in the early treaty to set the boundaries, obtaining thus the entire Forks of the Delaware—and something more. The final expulsion from the valley of its Indian occupants—three clans, the Munsey (Wolf totem) in the north, the Unamuni (Turtle) and the Unalachtgo (Turkey) in the south—was the inevitable sequel.

The Iroquois Council at Onondago had earlier assumed jurisdiction over the placid Lenape, once their 'elder brothers,' 'putting petticoats on

[13] Retribution followed swiftly—one of the runners dropped out from exhaustion, a second died of overexertion, the third was murdered by resentful Delawares.

[14] Certain pioneers along the upper Susquehanna—Fuchs, Rummerfeld, Schufeld—were possibly stragglers in this migration.

them, mortar and pestle in their hands,' forbidding them to fight, migrate, or sell their lands without permission, 'making women of them.' Now, with some caustic comment, they assigned their wards a refuge on the Susquehanna a hundred miles below Teaoga, a site to which the Iroquois had acquired title from the conquered Andaste or Susquehannocks. Here, where the Susquehanna breaks through the Blue Ridge, changing its course from easterly to westerly, the mountains sweep apart, leaving a great plain—Scahentoa or Quialamuck, later to become famous as the Wyoming Valley.[15] At this and other points along the North and West Branches of the Susquehanna the Lenni Lenape of the Delaware Valley, sullen, resentful of the trick turned upon them, took up their residence in 1742, under the leadership of a chief of the Turtle Clan, Teedyuscung, self-styled King of the Delawares.

This lovely central valley of the Susquehanna with its great hunting-grounds on the overhanging heights was a favorite Iroquoian haunt. Indian spokesmen for the Confederacy over and over again in sonorous accents declared they would never cede it to the whites, for 'there our bones lie buried,' and 'there our council-fires have burned since time immemorial.'[16]

In 1729, Conrad Weiser the Palatinate, whose family were leaders of the Schoharie group that passed Teaoga in 1723, followed with his wife Anna Eve and four small children, his father-in-law driving his stock along the bank where Sullivan's long cattle-train was to struggle fifty years later (in the reverse direction). Arrived at Womelsdorf, young Weiser soon made amends for the trouble with the Lenape his group had occasioned, proffering his services to the Province as interpreter and peacemaker with the Iroquois. For the star of the latter was now in the ascendant, that of the Lenape waning. Weiser's knowledge of the Mohawk tongue and ways, of the trails as well to Onondago, the seat of the Confederation's council-house, proved invaluable to his adopted country. Many a time in youth and age during the next quarter of a century he passed Teaoga, journeying to reach Onondago in the early spring 'before the shad-blow whitens on the hillside'—signal for war-parties to descend the Susquehanna. Deep snows, floods, near-starvation was his lot. Once he barely escaped drowning in the fierce Oscohu (Sugar Creek), and again in the wild currents of Tioga Branch (Chemung River). In his journal are many jottings on Teaoga, and on his Oneida comrade Shikellimy—along with hints that his old Mohawk foster-parent was better company than his own dour and disappointed father. Without question Conrad understood his Indian!

Assiduous travellers and frequent companions of Weiser, halting the night at Teaoga, were the religious exiles from Moravia—Zeisberger, Cammerhof, Spangenberg and Post—who in 1741 founded Bethlehem on the Lehigh; Salem in North Carolina in 1753; in 1765-72 missions among the Delaware Indians at Wyalusing, Tawandaemunk and Sheshequannunk, later transferred to Ohio. To these missions we probably owe the presence in our valley of Esther Montour, daughter of the famous French-Indian family that supplied us with so many friendly interpreters and guides.

---

[15] The first name is gutteral Andaste, the second the more liquid Lenape. The modern city of Wilkes Barre with its fringe of outlying communities—a total population of more than 150,000—is easily accommodated within this spacious valley. Anthracite-bearing strata outcrop in its mountain walls, the forested summits of which afford breezy summer residences and pleasure-grounds.

[16] See *The Thirteen Indian Treaties Printed by Benjamin Franklin 1736-62,* lately reissued by the Historical Society of Pennsylvania.

Esther came here from the West Branch as the wife of Egohowin, a Munsey (Delaware) chief.

Up the valley in 1743 in the company of Weiser and Shikellimy came the advance guard of civilization, the gentle self-taught Quaker botanist John Bartram, and geographer Lewis Evans, sent to reconnoitre and map the Susquehanna watershed for the British Crown. Their notes inform us not only of the trees and plants flourishing here, but of the ways also of the Indians living at Teaoga (sometimes called Tohiccon) in the early

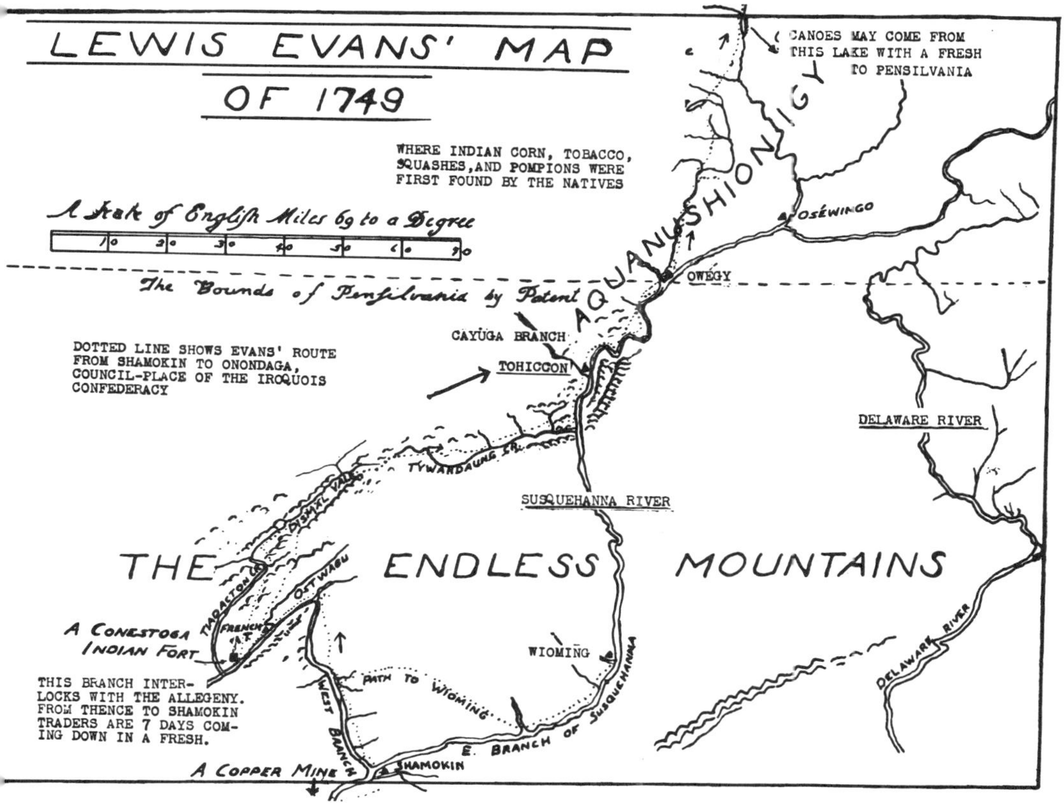

From Evans' Map of the Middle British Colonies

Showing Tohiccon at Junction of 'Tioga Branch' and Susquehanna on Bartram and Weiser's route to Onondaga, 1743

18th century—of the old squaw whose 'skin was like the bark of a tree', but whose cornbread and broth saved them from starvation.

Throughout the first half of this century and the French and Indian War, Sir William Johnson, Irishman, Indian agent for the Province of New York and later for the British Crown, labored valiantly with gifts and much palaver to keep the Iroquois from siding with the French.[17] Messengers kept the trails hot between Fort Stanwix and Onondago in the

[17] Johnson, after the death of his wife, took an Indian mate, Molly, sister of the famous Mohawk chief Joseph Brant, as mistress of his manor-house, where members of the Six Nations were lavishly entertained. Descendants of this union are said to have come to Frenchtown in 1793, later to northern Bradford County.

north, and Lancaster, Easton and Bethlehem in the south; and in lieu of embossed parchment or minted coins, wampum belts by the dozen passed from hand to hand. Teaoga, midway on the route, was halfway house for peace emissaries, or when all measures failed, campsite for war-parties launching raids on the Carolinas or the Wyoming or Cherry Valley, as entries in the Archives show.

Through the united efforts of Johnson, Shikellimy and Weiser, and many gifts, the crafty old chiefs at Onondago were persuaded to forego French alliance—a decision crucial for the continent. For presently, after the fall of Montreal and Quebec, France ceded her colonial possessions northward and westward as far as the Mississippi to the English Crown. All might have gone well, had the Delawares not got out of hand, stirred by new grievances.

Enter Connecticut and the Susquehannah Company

Penn's Province was as yet huddled in a triangular area along the Lehigh, Delaware and Schuylkill, in the southeast corner of the present Commonwealth, and our valley was still far beyond the frontier of actual settlement, when a new cloud arose on the horizon. Just at the moment when Indian groups driven in from the Hudson, Delaware, Chesapeake and Cumberland Valleys—Mohegans, Delawares, Nanticokes, Shawnee, Tutelos and Saponies—were finding asylum along the Susquehanna, the expanding colony of Connecticut resolved to exercise her charter privileges, stretching indefinitely westward between parallels 41 and 42.[18] Fixing her gaze on a portion of the Susquehanna valley due west of the Province, to be known henceforth as *Westmoreland*, and ignoring Penn's charter rights and Indian treaties, she sanctioned the Susquehannah Company. The latter recruited subscribers, and in 1753-4 persuaded four Indian chiefs (some say eighteen), for a considerable sum of money, to sign over a strip on either side of the Susquehanna; on the fertile lowlands of which 17 townships, each five miles square, and each to accommodate 50 families, were to be plotted. Surveyors were despatched at once—immediately resented by the Delawares in possession. Ironically, the forming of friendly Christian relations with these same Indians had been advanced as an argument to the Crown in favor of the Company!

The French and Indian War was on throughout the western borders, and with the now thoroughly aroused Lenape it was touch and go. Braddock's disaster in 1755 tipped the scales in favor of the French. Along the frontier of the Province, on the Mahoning and Penn's Creek, irate war-parties burned and scalped. A terrified girl captive, Susanna Nitchsman, of the same family as Count Zinzindorf's Moravian wife, was brought to Teaoga, where she died in 1756. Many other captives were held here enroute for Niagara. Their stories are recorded in the Archives.

The Delaware King Teedyuscung at Teaoga

To Teaoga in 1756-57 came the Delaware King and his subjects, ordered by the Iroquois to leave Wyoming 'for you are not fit to live with white people,' and obeying with an alacrity out of keeping with the clan

[18] Literal interpretation of this charter, fantastic even in the light of 1753 geographic knowledge, would have endowed Connecticut with a 3000-mile band reaching across the Rockies to the Pacific, and covering generous portions of ten future states. Ironically, this claim, entered by one of the most democratic of colonies, rested on the word of the long discredited and superseded Stuart kings.

totem. Here followed shortly messengers from the Governor of Pennsylvania, headed by 'Captain Newcastle,' Penn's Indian protegé, and a grand council was held at which the chiefs of all the nearby villages gathered. Teaoga (now Diahoga), it will be recalled, was the deadline of hostilities set by our Province, Johnson holding his Iroquois in leash above.

A long series of councils followed, at Easton, Lancaster and elsewhere, with journeys to the north and to the Ohio also. Since Teedyuscung in the end saw fit to tip the scales for peace and the cause of the English crown, and since he paid for this complaisance later with his life, he has received some eulogy in early histories. A later writer calls him 'a black-hearted rascal.' After scanning the records, we are inclined to suspend judgment.

While waiting for some local Shakespeare to put this many-faceted, tragico-comic character, this roystering, braggart 'King of Ten Nations' on the boards, we may cull a few delicious bits from his saga. Such are his demands that 'good tobacco, several horseloads of provisions, and a little Dram,' be provided against his arrival; and later that a horse, a European uniform and a gold-laced hat be added. At the council, he demanded a secretary in the English style, as 'a king's due,' refusing to rely as had his ancestors on the compendious memory of his race, or on the notes kept for the Governor. Choicest of all we find the King's parting gift to 'Brother Onas'—literally *Brother Pen*— 'fifteen deerskins to make him some gloves' —a delicate bit of satire of which the Indian was not incapable. At the Council he had harped continually on the unfair wresting of land from the Delawares by the Province.[19]

The arithmetic of Teedyuscung was not above suspicion. Like Prince Hal's crony at the Boar's Head Tavern, he was better at multiplying than at dividing. The Ten Nations he claimed as his subjects have never been listed. Though he appears to have rallied delegates from all but the Munseys at the councils, the Iroquois indignantly repudiated his authority to represent them. These many and prolonged council gatherings, attended by a numerous and riotous throng, to the distress of staid Bethlehem, halfway house on the journey, appear to have been mainly for the purpose of marking time, and levying tribute—supplies were scarce at deserted and unplanted Diahoga. Curiously, Captain Newcastle, Penn's protegé, envoy to Teedyuscung at Diahoga, claimed at Easton that the Delawares—a nation of medicine men—had bewitched him. Falling ill, first of pleurisy, later of smallpox, he died of the latter. Should this be set in the score against Teedyuscung?

Usually 'in his cups,' voluble and truculent, this 'aboriginal Falstaff' was capable of complete abstinence and instant sobriety when weightier matters pended, as in the case of the long peace journey to the western Indians. Animated by a double grievance, his two dispossessions, he set the price of allegiance to the English high—the building of a white man's town and home for himself and followers precisely on the contested site, Wyoming. His choice had better have fallen on Teaoga. For five years only, from 1758-63, he enjoyed possession. Whether a Connecticut claimant or an

---

[19] Teedyuscung is described as tall, muscular, raw-boned, moody, fond of fine clothes and rum, with a wild company of followers, the women wearing skirts of Dutch tablecloths. He was 'convicted of sin by Moravian preaching' and baptised, but proved an unstable convert. Resentful of wrongs, he is credited with arraying the Indians against the English early in the French-Indian War, later—for a price—restraining them. See O.T.P., 75 ff.

Iroquois agent set fire to his house, cremating him in its ruins, is a matter of speculation.

What was happening along the Susquehanna in the latter days of Teedyuscung's sway? In 1762-63, in a lull in the Indian wars—just before Pontiac raised the hatchet in the north—a number of share-holders of the Susquehannah Company had again migrated to the Wyoming Valley. Fortified by the belief that they were the chosen of God and destined to inherit the earth, they staked out their claims, cleared their acres and reared their log-cabins. While the resulting conflicts of these Yankees with the protesting officials and forces of Penn from Lancaster and Philadelphia, and the reprisals of outraged Indians on their outlying cabins lay far below Teaoga, reverberations of course stirred our little peninsula, the usual detention-place of captives.

Much of our knowledge of the middle century is drawn from the journals of the Moravians who maintained missions along the upper Susquehanna in 1765-72—when Teaoga was all but deserted. On their earlier mid-century trips as many as fifty cabins were reported here, and war-parties of four to five hundred. The tribes represented, their manners, religious rites and customs are minutely noted. We can see in fancy's eye the Mohegans (by no means the last) smoking their long pipes around the fire on the Point, eating their scanty ration of watery squash broth, corn-cake and maple sugar in time of famine. We can share also in fatter times the hospitality of the Cayuga village near Spanish Hill, faring on such delicacies as roast bear's haunch, dried eels, and huckleberry cake. We learn of the virtues of the sweat-bath—the medicine-man's compound of mental suggestion and practical therapy.[20] The Indian's reverence for the sun, his invocation with tobacco and smoke of the spirits of waterfall and torrent, are set down also, with some cynical evangelical comment. We find gnats, canker worms in the corn, serpents, and rifts in the river ascribed to the invention of the Evil One. Paintings on the tree-trunks depicting the passage of war-parties are described also.

A lay brother attending Post records unsympathetically at Diahoga:

> This day the Indians began to Sacrifice to their God, and spent the day in a very odd manner, howling and dancing, raveling like wolves and painted frightful as Devils.

These were probably Munseys of the Wolf Clan.

About this time also the dream-mongering Delawares at Diahoga reported a strange vision in the moon. None dared venture to interpret the portent, nor has any since made bold to identify the contestants. Two horses had appeared, one from the east, one from the west, contending fiercely until the eastern stallion bore down and drove out the western. Did the struggle forecast the triumph of St. George's charger over St. Louis' and the peace of Paris? The ultimate victory in Westmoreland of Connecticut Puritan over Pennsylvania Quaker? Or the coming of some yet unheralded disaster out of the East? None knows.

Esther Montour and Her Munseys Settle on the Flats

Much of local interest may be gleaned from the testimony of white captives held here on a diet of fish and wild berries, and forced to run the gauntlet between lines of Indian women and children armed with sticks and stones. To one Jane Strope, captured at Wysox, we owe the true story

[20] The sweatbath treatment, followed by a plunge in an icy creek, was adopted with success by our early local doctors.

of the much maligned Queen Esther, whose 'palace' stood across the river from the Point until Hartley burned it in 1778. Esther, granddaughter of Madame Montour (French-Indian from Quebec who lived on the West Branch, giving modern Montoursville its name) had not only Huron but also Oneida and Mohawk chieftains' blood in her veins.

Married to Egohowin, a Munsey chief displaced from the Delaware to old Sheshewannuck, where the trail from the West Branch came in, and where a Moravian mission had located in 1769, Esther left on Egohowin's death in 1772. When the Christian Delawares at Wyalusing and other points along the river relinquished their uncertain tenure and departed

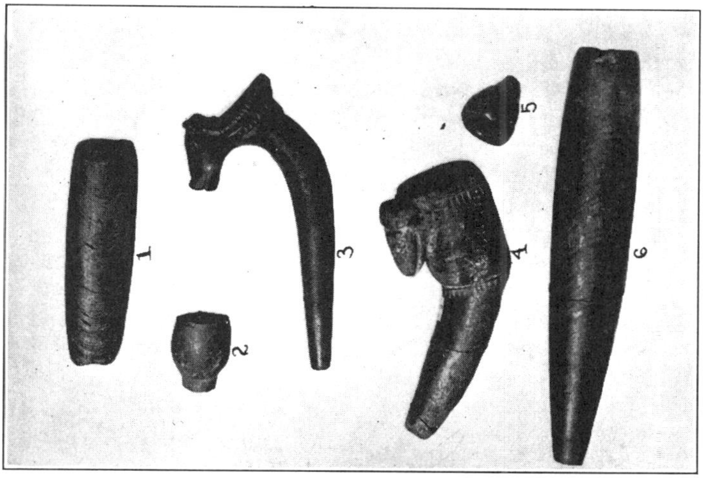

WOLF PIPE FROM ESTHER'S MUNSEY VILLAGE
With steatite tubes used by Delaware medicine-men to simulate removal from patient of cause of illness

mournfully under Zeisberger's leadership for the Ohio, Esther with a small group of her husband's Munseys moved to the five-mile flats that still carry her name. (These were part of the Iroquois grant to the Moravian missions in 1766, which extended up past Teaoga.) Here her two sisters, Mary and Catherine, who had married Seneca chiefs, sometimes visited her. On the terrace between Wolcott's and Buck's creeks where stood her 'palace' a baked-clay pipe with a well-modelled wolf's head has been recovered in our day, reminding us that the totem of her husband's clan, the Munsey, was a wolf.[21]

French Margaret, Esther's mother, is rumored to have been with her at times at Teaoga, when the valley was shunned by all but the Wolf Clan from Wilawana to Wyalusing, Nanticoke and Shawnee under old Paxinosa having passed on to other points. The Munseys alone of all the Delawares turned a cold shoulder to Teedyuscung's latter pleas for peace with the English colonies, favoring the French cause even after it was lost. Margaret, rumoured to have been the granddaughter of an old French governor, may have been acting as a French agent. The Montours had long served the English colonies loyally as interpreters, and had been made much of, Margaret having once

[21] The Indian felt close kinship with the animal kingdom, each group accepting some one species as ancestral mascot. Deer, bear, beaver, raccoon, turtle, snipe, heron, turkey, and hawk were among these 'totems'; often used by chiefs as pictographic signatures to treaties (see facsimile in the Museum), and as models for imitation by the youth of the tribe. The turtle, it may be added, is important in Indian mythology, fabled as holding up the earth.

visited New York in state, with six packhorses and an Irish groom. Perhaps, however, French blood and knowledge of the French tongue drew them back to the long forsworn allegiance at a time when Pennsylvania's governor was extending scant courtesy to his Indian wards on the upper Susquehanna.

According to Jane Strope (later Mrs. Gideon Whittaker), Esther herself was a tall commanding woman, dressed in blue broadcloth with many silver ornaments and bells, who connived at the escape of many captives at nearby Teaoga; saw also that the victims of Indian wrath were decently interred. With what mixed feelings she looked on at the gathering of Butler's Rangers in their gay green uniforms, Macdonald and his 400 painted Iroquois, for the descent on Wyoming in 1778, we cannot guess. An unfortunate incident before the attack, however, brought her fierce Mohawk blood to the fore. For Indian ethics demanded that the death of her boy, killed in a skirmish above Exeter, be properly avenged. Hence she has come down in history as perpetrator of the tomahawking of 14 white prisoners—the requisite number of commoners to atone for the loss of a chief's son. In the actual battle or massacre she had no part, but to the families of the fourteen victims she remains 'the she-devil of Wyoming.'

Her village was abandoned before Hartley reached it in his reprisal raid of 1778. Whether she joined her sister Catherine at Catherine's Town at the head of Seneca Lake, or went elsewhere, or where she is buried remains a mystery. How she came to be called Queen Esther we can only guess. History should set her down, however, as the white man's friend, many degrees less bloodthirsty than her Old Testament prototype.

At the opening of the Revolution there were still Tutelos on Tutelo Creek, Munseys at Esther's Flats, Cayugas possibly west of Spanish Hill or in the Old Indian Fields of South Waverly; with other settlements at Chemung, Wilawana, Sugar Creek. The Indian had blazed the way for his white successor with his apple orchards and sugar groves, his cleared fields of corn and bean and squash—the "Three Sisters." His trails up and down the rivers and creeks and across to the Delaware were worn deep—pointing the way to highways and railroads to come.[22] The technique of his corncribs and his sugaring-off, his domestication of the dog, lay open to white copy. Many of his tools—celts, scrapers, pestles—were used in pioneering households. His canoe was the accepted mode of transportation.

Indian Myths and Legends of the Valley

If George Catlin,[23] born at Wilkes Barre (early Wyoming) fitly became the painter of the Indian in picturesque war-garb, it is equally fitting that Teaoga should have given his start in life to one Guy Maxwell, clerk at Hollenback's trading-post from 1788-95 and grandfather of Harriet Maxwell Converse. For this troubled eighteenth century, with its many councils of peace and war, at which Indian guests must be fed and humored with numerous gifts, had brought traders into the upper valley. Anderson the Quaker in 1763 to Sheshequannock, with its Munseys; in 1768, Secord to Tenghannock, later to Teaoga—where he cleared seven acres from river to river at the Academy site; Matthias Hollenback to Wilkes Barre in 1769; in 1783, when Secord the Tory had been driven from Teaoga, to our valley

[22] The Great Warrior, Sheshequin and Minnisink Paths, down the Susquehanna, across country to the West Branch, and from Teaoga east to the Delaware.

[23] A character borrowed and transplanted to New England by Kenneth Roberts in *Northwest Passage*.

and to Newtown above (later Elmira).[24] Guy Maxwell was an early clerk of Hollenback's at Teaoga, (as was also Stephen Tuttle, another Elmira pioneer), and secretary at many treaty councils.

Harriet Maxwell, whose father was born at Teaoga (old Tioga Point or Athens), early befriended the Indian, was adopted into an Iroquois tribe, as had been her father and her grandfather before her, and collected the tales and legends of the Seneca, probably varying little from those of our own Andastes.[25] Through her we learn of the yearly Indian festivals and dances—the Maple Sugar and Strawberry Festivals, the Green Corn Planting and Harvest Feasts—in all of which magical ceremonies designed to influence and direct nature spirits appear to have mingled with thanks-

THE FLYING HEAD
Indian Myth of the Whirlwind

giving. We learn also of the medical fraternity (the False-Face Society); and of the Flying Heads—wind spirits, visible even in our day in the cloud-shapes above Spanish Hill, southwest of which a mild tornado once laid low the forest. Another local legend of a horned monster dwelling in the caves of the hills may owe its origin to the tusks of the mammoth found embedded in the banks of the Chemung.

Today those of us whose ancestors were neither scalped or tortured may agree to let oblivion fall on the old tales of Indian atrocities (provoked too often by treacherous white treatment, scalp bounties, and the unregu-

[24] As early as 1761 Indian chieftains had asked for a trading-post at Diahoga, where they might buy ammunition—the sale of rum to be definitely prohibited. Concentrated alcohol was a novelty to the Indian, who rarely practised moderation in its use, regarding it as a semi-magical decoction of hearts, brains and tongues, stimulating all these organs. Only the old chiefs or those reared by the Moravians knew better.

[25] Printed in 1908 by the New York State Museum. Recently issued in modernized version by another woman friend of the Indian as *Legends of the Long House Told by Jesse Cornplanter*, 1938.

lated rum traffic); turning more profitably to assay the skilled craftsmanship, the humor and kindliness to children, the food and cultural gifts, and the imaginative nature myths and legends of our Indian predecessors, many of whose descendants are good Americans.

First, however, we have to traverse a long and painful chapter in our annals. * * * In 1768, at Fort Stanwix, a strip from 'Owegy' to the mouth of 'Tawandee,' *covering most of our valley*, was formally released by its Iroquois owners to the Province of Pennsylvania. Ominously, in 1775, the Susquehannah Company of Connecticut laid out its seventeenth township, *Ulster*, overlapping Teaoga almost to Spanish Hill.

II. TIOGA POINT IN THE REVOLUTIONARY WAR: THE HARTLEY AND SULLIVAN EXPEDITIONS AND THE FORT AT TEAOGA

He who rides may read today the story of Sullivan's great five months' campaign, as crucial in our War of Independence as Saratoga, told in bronze and granite along hundreds of miles of superb modern highway. Across the Pocono plateau from the Delaware to the Susquehanna, where a detachment toiled in the early summer of 1779 through marsh and forest, past dense rhododendron thickets and snake-infested ledges—fitly dubbed 'the Shades of Death'—runs the trail.[1] Up the east side of the Susquehanna, twisting in its defile of wooded hills, its rocky narrows alternating with fertile flats, another line of markers stretches.[2] From Teaoga, site of Sullivan's Fort, a third series, under the caption Sullivan-Clinton Campaign, ascends the Chemung or 'Tioga Branch,' passing the Newtown battlefield, and crosses the divide to Seneca Lake; continuing thence up the east shore, and westward from lake to lake of the legendary Iroquois Long House, to terminate in Genesee Castle, stronghold of the dreaded Seneca chieftain Little Beard. In our valley alone there are half a dozen markers and boulders, the earliest set in 1902, through the initiative of the Tioga Point Chapter of the Daughters of the American Revolution, the local historical society, and later of the Pennsylvania Historical Commission.

The epic progress of this wilderness trek, comparable only with Sherman's March to the Sea or the blazing of the Oregon Trail, is told in tattered and faded diaries also, and in the books of orderlies, several of which Tioga Point Museum published in 1903 and 1929. Notable among them are those of Thomas Gee and of Colonel Francis Barber, great-uncle of Henry and William James. Not for a hundred years, however, was the full meaning of Sullivan's 'raid' in breaking Iroquois support of the British army, and camouflaging Washington's plan to transfer his campaign to Virginia, fully realised by the historian.[3] Fifty years more were to pass before the route was adequately marked.[4]

A poster of the first Centennial, which the gifted historian, David Craft, did much to promote, is preserved by the Museum, along with

[1] From Easton to Wilkes Barre.

[2] The modern highway shortcuts inland over breezy knolls.

[3] Disappointed because Niagara and Detroit were not attacked, the general public failed to sense the magnitude of the task actually accomplished in an unmapped wilderness, with a minimum of loss. Perhaps our legislators smarted also under the leader's tart criticism of delays in furnishing supplies and men. Adversely criticized on every hand, Sullivan resigned his command and returned to the law.

[4] Eloquently advocated for a quarter of a century by William Elliot Griffis.

cannon balls and bullets culled from local gardens, flintlock, powder-horn, bullet-mould, spy-glass and other articles that played their part in the Expedition of 1779.[5]

To our Valley, the import of the 'raid' was more than military. The tattered drummers, riflemen and boatmen who pushed through the uncharted wilderness with Indians hanging on flank and rear, through the sweltering heats, the pelting rains and fogs of midsummer, hailed it as a scouting expedition into Canaan. Intermixed in their journals with gory tales of scalpings, disciplinary floggings, accidental shootings, and drownings and collapse from overexertion, are eloquent eulogies of winding river glimpsed from rocky hillsides, of fertile flats where the grasses overtopped a man's head. Many an officer and private under Hartley or Sullivan returned when war was over to stake out a claim on some river terrace, forested slope or green creek valley that had caught his fancy while he guided his packhorse along slippery narrows, poled his boat with its cargo of cannon or provender against the current, herded the cattle on Esther's flats or chased marauding Indians over Round Top. Incredibly, one lucky survivor conceived an undying ardor for a certain green glade where his Indian captors bound him preliminary to torture.

The Opening of the Revolutionary Era: Battle and Massacre of Wyoming

What of our Valley at the outset of the Revolution? Toward which side did our Indian occupants and scattered pioneers incline, and where lay the frontier of the thirteen rebellious colonies? In 1775 the province of New York was confined to the Hudson and lower Mohawk valleys. Its western frontier ran from present Utica to Binghamton. Beyond lay unbroken forest, a great game-stocked plateau with its thirteen fingerlike lakes, its waterways running east, west, north, and south, dominating the northeast quarter of the continent. Hidden in the forest were islets of Iroquoian cornfields, orchards and longhouses.

Pennsylvania still was huddled in the southeast corner of her present boundaries, between the Delaware and Schuylkill, in a four-county area behind a four-county frontier—though since the Indian Purchase of 1768 three more great sprawling counties had been laid out on her northwestern border. Since 1763, however, when French cession of all claims east of the Mississippi removed danger from the west, the Connecticut shareholders of the Susquehannah Company had begun to flock into 'Westmoreland,' the western province along the Susquehanna claimed by virtue of king's grant and Indian purchase. Alluvial lowlands were especially alluring now that Connecticut's thin soils were depleted by careless farming. Seventeen townships, each five miles square, were laid out along the river from Huntington (Nescopeck) to Ulster—to be a thorn in the flesh alike of the Penns, who claimed sole right to grant manors here, and of the Iroquois Council, who refused to confirm the sale by a handful of chiefs at Albany to the Susquehannah Company.

The rage of Iroquois and Lenni Lenape alike at this white intrusion on their favorite hunting ground unquestionably played a central rôle in the Wyoming Massacre, in the year preceding Sullivan's Expedition. For Quialaumuck, the beautiful Wyoming Valley, granted by the Iroquois to their wards the Lenape in compensation for the Delaware (lost by the in-

[5] Copies of soldiers' diaries and other source material are preserved in the Craft Collection of the Museum.

famous Walking Purchase), and often declared inalienable ground, never to be ceded to the whites, was the focal area in the Susquehannah Company's settlement of their purchase.[6]

The cool head and firm grip of Conrad Weiser, Indian mediator, and of his ally, the friendly Oneida Shikellimy, had long been missing at the helm of Indian affairs. Sir William Johnson was dead. The younger Johnsons, and Joseph Brant the Mohawk, after his reception at London by the King, and the flattery of a portrait by the celebrated Romney, swung the Confederacy to the side of the Crown—the Great White Father across seas, their traditional allegiance. The Iroquois Long House became the main granary and garden of the British army, Tories and soldiers of the line working side by side with Indian women in the cornfields.

Driven from the lower Mohawk by our victory at Saratoga, British officers at Fort Niagara and Oswego recruited from Tory settlers throughout the countryside the band known as Butler's Rangers. These worked hand in hand with their Iroquois allies, are said to have doffed at times their gay green uniforms for Indian war-paint and feathers, when a raid on our frontiers was in order. By 1778-9 all supporters of the Continental cause were driven far southward along the Susquehanna, and the Tory Secord was established at Teaoga.[7] Seven acres were cleared at the 'neck,' a deep well dug, a storehouse built, and Secord the hunter and trapper became a sutler for the British at Niagara or passing war-parties, collecting and storing corn or cattle. After defeat at Ticonderoga cut the British off from the Hudson, the regular route for Brant's Mohawk clansmen was down the Susquehanna from headquarters at Oghwago (Windsor), across the carry or portage at Teaoga, and up the Chemung to Ft. Niagara. Already the British were casting envious eyes further, on the mid-Susquehanna cornfields, harvests sorely needed by troops quartered on New York City.

Intimate details bearing on this period may be found in the testimony of four Pennsylvania girls who were either taken captive by the Indians, or caught in the vortex of events. They are: Elizabeth Satterlee, who was in the thick of the massacre of Wyoming, fleeing through the woods with an invalid mother who died of exhaustion. Later as Mrs. Elisha Matthewson of Athens, she told her story to her descendants, some of whom are still among us.[8] So did Hannah Gore, later Mrs. Elisha Durkee, daughter of blacksmith Obadiah who removed from Wyoming to Queen Esther's Flats, and later to Sheshequin, to become a pioneer judge, and acquire fame as the first to use anthracite coal as fuel, and one of the ablest diarists of Sullivan's Expedition. Jane Strope of Wysox (later Mrs. Gideon Whittaker) is the third detained by captors for a period at Teaoga on a diet of wild berries. Mary Jemison from Marsh Creek far down the Susquehanna was the fourth. Of Scotch-Irish descent, adopted by a Seneca, and married to three Indian chiefs in turn, she refused to leave her Indian family when located at the close of the war. In old age she gave to the press a graphic

---

[6] A strip 120-mile wide between the 41st and 42nd parallels was claimed. More than a hundred townships east and west of the Susquehanna are sketched on an old map in the Museum, inscribed with quaint classical names.

[7] Others in the neighborhood were Daniel Moore who ran a ferry across the Susquehanna, and Provost, whose 'plantation' lay somewhere below Spanish Hill.

[8] Her portrait in austere old age, by some local Rembrandt, dominates the Colonial Room of the Museum.

narrative of the Iroquois retreat before General Sullivan's advance northward,[9] which has passed through many editions.

From Jane Strope we have the picture of the British and their savage allies gathering on the site of the Spalding Museum-Library, while a fleet of canoes and boats was built nearby for the descent on Wyoming. Early in July after a white dog feast and dancing the joint expedition started, Butler's Rangers gay in their green uniforms with buff facings, their caps with the glittering gilt letters R.G. (Rex Georgius); the Iroquois in red and black striped war paint. The combined force is said to have numbered about a thousand.

Harvesting parties in the upper Wyoming Valley were caught in a surprise attack on the outlying forts July 3, 1778. The refusal of the little garrison at Forty-Fort to surrender, the consequent massacre of the men and flight of the women and children[10] over the mountains to the Delaware or down to Sunbury, their way lit by the flare of burning homesteads, is an oft-told tale.[11] One woman sat resolutely on the chest that contained her wedding finery, only to see her white satin bonnet worn off in triumph by an Indian before whose tomahawk her courage finally wavered.

Two hundred were widowed in the three days carnage, and the Wyoming Valley was for a time deserted. Many families who afterward emigrated to our valley suffered. Seven men of the Gore family which later settled in Sheshequin were victims. A small folding table that escaped the pillage; feathers scattered from a bed slit by the plundering Indians, and retrieved from an angle of a stump fence; a fragment of the Bloody Rock around which (legend tells us) were ranged the fourteen white captives chosen to atone for the killing of Queen Esther's son, are among the souvenirs of this sanguinary Revolutionary episode conserved in the Museum. Homes and barns were burned, and much plunder taken, including 300 head of cattle driven off to Sheshequin and Teaoga.

The country rang with tales of this disaster and its accompanying horrors, before which the old Deerfield massacre paled. Ironically, the inadequate defence of the Wyoming Forts was due in part to the summoning of local military groups to the standard of the remote mother state Connecticut!

Colonel Hartley's Expedition of 1778 to Teaoga

With Wyoming desolate and abandoned, Indian vengeance centered on the West Branch, settlers from which, shortly after the Wyoming disaster, stampeded down the river in the Great Runaway. Piteous appeals for aid were made to Pennsylvania, Connecticut and Congress. Though troops were desperately needed elsewhere, Colonel Thomas Hartley of the 11th Pennsylvania Regiment, a 31-year old lawyer from Berks County, was despatched to Sunbury (Fort Augusta). Seven hundred men were placed at his disposal, to safeguard the frontiers, and protect the hardy pioneers returning to garner the much-needed harvest. Chafing a little at the commission to fight savages rather than British troops of the line, the young officer conceived a bold design. He would forestall attack and intimidate

---

[9] See J. E. Seaver, *Mary Jemison*, 1835. In Letchworth Park (northwestern New York), a fine statue commemorates her vigorous womanhood and leadership. Her descendants may still be found on the Cornplanter Reservation in western Pennsylvania.

[10] Women and children were not molested personally, according to agreement, though many perished of hunger or exposure.

[11] Celebrated somewhat too lushly and lacrimosely by the poet Campbell in *Gertrude of Wyoming*.

the enemy by a dash into their own country—hardly less hazardous than the sally of Rogers' Rangers up the St. Francis (the harrowing details of which are narrated in Kenneth Roberts' *Northwest Passage*).

Hartley's raid, overshadowed by Sullivan's, is known to us mainly through his own terse but eloquent Report to Congress, and his letters to his comrade-in-arms and fellow-Pennsylvanian, General Anthony Wayne. Building as a base Fort Muncy on the West Branch (a fine model of which is on display at the new Muncy Museum), commandeering cannon for it, Hartley set as his objectives the Indian settlements at Teaoga and Chemung. A native of the Conrad Weiser sector, reared on tales of the old interpreter's wilderness journeys, he chose the difficult, overgrown Sheshequin Path, traversed by Conrad in 1737, for a surprise approach. The Susquehanna above Tunkhannock was, he knew, in the hands of Indian and Tory.

The start from Fort Muncy was made at 4 A.M. September 21, with but 200 of the 400 men promised, 17 light horse, rations for 12 days only, and 100 rounds of ammunition. Illness had delayed the takeoff until the equinoctial rains set in. Three days were spent in traversing the morasses and rocky ledges, the maze of fallen tree-trunks and frost-split boulders of the wild Lycoming Gorge, its waters swollen by heavy rains.[12] Only those who essayed the passage of a like defile, with its narrow trail obliterated by rising waters, fording a dozen times a mile through swirling currents, clambering over boulders and half-rotten logs, sinking into mossy pitfalls, climbing cliffs on hands and knees with a perilous handgrip on hemlock or maple saplings, can frame any notion of the advance of Hartley's forces through the downpour, heavily laden with musket, knapsack and bullet pouch. Everywhere were grewsome signs of the recent passage of the savage foe, their smouldering fires, 'the huts where they had dressed their scalps.' In the clipped, vivid phrases of his reports the young attorney (who knew his Latin) likens the hazards of the ascent with Hannibal's passage of the Alps.

Drenched, yet fearful of lighting fires to dry their clothing, the men emerged near picturesque Cedar Ledge, and crossed the Beaver Meadow swamp toward the headwaters of Towanda. Somewhere between present Canton and LeRoy (site of a former Indian village) there was a brush with an Indian party, who withdrew with the body of their leader, sending runners on to warn the encampments above. Crossing the low divide to Sugar Creek near Burlington, and following the valley almost to the site of ancient Ogehage, Hartley and his little band forded Hemlock Run, and pushed up the Susquehanna past Old Sheshequin.[13] Only to find Queen Esther's and Teaoga, on the Point across the river, deserted in the dusk! On this their sixth day they had covered 22 miles, reaching the junction of 'Tioga Branch' with the Susquehanna, just below the famous Carry and Tory rendezvous.

At Teaoga, to Hartley's grievous disappointment, the expected union with Morgan's Light-Horse, then attached to General James Clinton's New York brigade, was not effected. The report from Captain Carberry, who

---

12 Now traversed by the Northern Central R.R.

13 Called 'Calabash Town,' from the gourds used as medicine man's rattles. Here six short years before the Moravian missionary Roth, living in the house of the Quaker trader, Anderson, had labored among Joe Peepe's Christian Delawares and Echobund's Pagans—vainly translating the gospel of peace into a Delaware dialect. 'Sheep' and 'goats' occupied opposite sides of what is now Cash Creek.

with his 17 horsemen had pushed on beyond Tutelo village, that Butler's Rangers and a band of Indians 500 strong were gathering at Chemung 12 miles above, rendered speedy retreat down the river with the plunder the only prudent course. Not only had the Indian cabins at Teaoga,[14] Queen Esther's, and Sheshequin been burnt, 28 canoes were captured, 15 prisoners

Queen Esther's Village Marker
On East of Highway at Greene's Landing below Athens

released, and a portion of the spoils from Wyoming retrieved—cattle and packhorses.

Crossing the Susquehanna below Old Sheshequin, in a forced march of 28 miles down the east bank they passed safely the ancient Indian lookout on Wyalusing Rocks and reached the lowland site of the old Moravian Mission town at 11 P.M. September 28. Flour supplies were exhausted, and they were forced to delay till near noon the next day to slaughter and

[14] The expedition appears, however, to have missed Secord the sutler's storehouse at the Neck.

roast beef for the balance of the journey. Putting to the torch the last remnants of the little agricultural colony of Papunhank and Job Chilloway,[15] they pushed on again—but the delay had given the enemy an advantage in the pursuit.

On Browntown Mountain (September 28) there were two sharp frontal skirmishes, and on Indian Hill (north of Tuscarora Creek and present Laceyville) flank and rear engagement with 200 Indians, in which, though he lost four men killed and 11 wounded, Hartley put the enemy to flight—advancing with clamour and shouting, reinforced by the 70 footsore men who had taken to the boats. In action with Hartley were Captains Simon Spalding and John Franklin, and Lieutenants John Jenkins and Obadiah Gore, (all of whom we shall meet again) as well as a number of seasoned Indian fighters, notably Captains Brady and Murray. Two more days found the party at Wyoming with the plunder (promptly put to auction). With his tattered, ill-rationed 200, their leader had completed a circuit of nearly three hundred miles in less than two weeks, taken 50 head of cattle and burned four villages.

Shortly thereafter, the Indians struck again from their rendezvous at Teaoga (where Jane Strope's captors remained concealed through Hartley's raid), carrying off from the Wyoming Valley little Frances Slocum into lifelong captivity; bringing destruction on Cherry Valley near the headwaters of the Susquehanna. But the work of Hartley's Expedition was done. The trail was blazed for a more portentous advance. Hartley's insistence on the need of an Indian campaign of *horsemen* (for an Indian can outrun a white man); of *noise and shouting* (4 musicians accompanied him, 142 were requisitioned for the succeeding expedition), and of *cannon*, to destroy savage morale; of the precaution of *scouting parties* on flank and rear and in the van—proved invaluable at headquarters. Further, he had shown that the old Sheshequin Path up the Lycoming was impracticable for the requisite army and equipment.

The four Indian settlements, with their outlying cornfields, to which this dashing young commander gave the *coup de grace*, were never rebuilt. Markers at and near Athens indicate the position of century-old Teaoga on the Point and Queen Esther's more recent Munsey colony (2.2 miles below the Tioga St. bridge on the highway). On the breezy heights of Browntown Mountain, (Indian Hill) commanding one of the finest panoramas of the valley, with its line on line of misty azure hills, a third marker commemorates Hartley's engagement with the Indians, said to be the liveliest fought in Bradford County in historic times. Here Sullivan's men found grisly relics of the battle—a skull hanging on a tree, and some battered Queen Anne muskets.

Sullivan's Expedition: May to October 1779

Sullivan's Campaign has at last taken its place in history, as the major event of the year 1779—otherwise notable for the brilliant exploits of Anthony Wayne on the Hudson, and John Paul Jones on the British coast. To eliminate the Indian menace in the rear, cut off the British from the great granaries of the Iroquois Confederacy, and safeguard the harvest-

[15] Where once the chapel bell had summoned to Christian worship. For here the devoted Moravian missionary and linguist David Zeisberger had set down the strange heathen rites of his charges in the 'Wyalusing Diary,' compiled his dictionary of the Delaware tongue, and laid his vain plans for a Christian Indian state, devoted to the propagation of peace (1769 to 1772).

fields of the Susquehanna for our own forces, was worth detaching four brigades and their commanders—one-third of the total strength of the Continental army—in the opinion of the Commander-General. Master of strategy, Washington planned to hold his main campaign in check, duping the enemy with carefully feinted moves, until this masterstroke in the west was achieved to his satisfaction.

Hartley's reports were minutely studied, and individuals of many types with a knowledge of the back country interrogated—hunters, surveyors, traders, officers, deserters.[16] Result, a threefold plan, for advance from Schenectady, Fort Pitt and Wyoming, with Teaoga as the main point of union—thence a bold destructive foray at harvest time through the heart of the Iroquois country. Brigadier-Generals Enoch Poor and William Maxwell were to proceed across the Poconos from the Wind Gap on the Delaware to Wyoming, with New Hampshire, Massachusetts and New Jersey regiments. For this was no mere local stroke of reprisal, but an integral part of the main campaign, of vital moment to the common cause.

At Wyoming General Edward Hand's Light Horse (the companies of two of Hartley's experienced captains, John Franklin's and Simon Spaulding's among them) would assemble,[17] along with Colonel Thomas Proctor's Artillery and military band. For Hartley's stress on the imperative need of *horsemen, cannon, riflemen* and *noise* in dealing with a savage foe went not unheeded. Hartley's seasoned fighters would serve also under Lieut.-Colonel Adam Hubley.[18] Their gallant leader of 1778, probably never fully recovered from the stresses and hardships of his daring sally,[19] had resigned command to accept office in the Pennsylvania Assembly, later in Congress.

Advancing from Schenectady up the Mohawk and across to Otsego Lake, headwaters of the Susquehanna, Brigadier-General James Clinton's command were instructed to descend the river by boat to Teaoga, where the main expeditionary force and supplies would await them. Meanwhile Colonel Daniel Brodhead was to advance from Fort Pitt, with several hundred of his garrison.

The command of the Expedition was first tendered to General Gates as senior officer, but passed by him to Major-General John Sullivan, obviously Washington's real choice. A sturdy, brave, resourceful, and eloquent Irish lawyer, already seasoned in the service, who put through the campaign planned by Washington with aplomb, in the face of untold odds. Lagging and insufficient supplies, reluctantly granted or withheld by Congress, a tremendous baggage train to convoy along narrow trails through an unmapped wilderness, motley troops as yet unsure of the wisdom of advance beyond their respective bailiwicks, plus the disconcerting antics of a desperate savagery, dodging and hiding in the virgin forest, were among the trials the General met unflinchingly, though often with tart comment.

Scantily provisioned and poorly clothed, a force numbering about

---

[16] The questionary and summary of results is still in existence.

[17] With the expedition also was the young French volunteer with his flying company, Armand, Marquis de La Rouerie; young John Jenkins, Lieut. Obadiah Gore, and Major Adam Hoops of Carlyle, the last three of whom were destined to play prominent rôles in the development of this section.

[18] Who was to illustrate his Journal of the Western Expedition with invaluable sketches of the halts. A map of Sullivan's route from Wyoming to Teaoga, and from Fort Sullivan to the Genesee, showing the exact location of all halts, was painstakingly compiled for the Museum in 1937.

[19] Both Hartley and Sullivan died in the early fifties.

3500, inclusive of the 450 boatmen, 142 fifers and drummers, the 'pioneers' (axmen), and a number of women cooks, laundresses and nurses, with their children set out from Wyoming July 31, 1779. The ten precious cannon—3-, 4- and 6-pounders, and two small howitzers—along with the heavier supplies, barrels of flour and meat, were poled and rowed laboriously up 100 miles of winding river on hundreds of great bateaux secured from Marietta. Crashing through the forest along steep wooded hillsides, splashing through oozy lowland swamps, wound the vast column of 1200 pack-horses (none too steady on their ancient legs, if the tales of Horseheads are to be credited). The 800 head of cattle were herded at the center, with horsemen guarding van and rear and flanks as best they might in the dense undergrowth. "General Sullivan did not prepare to be Braddocked," comments one historian.

Meanwhile, from lookouts overhead, small bands of savage warriors spied sullenly on the advance of doom, now and then seizing and scalping unwary sentinels or herdsmen. Morning and evening, cannon were fired to intimidate the skulkers. In one such sunset salute, a corner of the great Standing Stone below Wysox was (perhaps deliberately) cracked off. This stone had been an Indian landmark for centuries, is said once to have been engraved with Indian pictographs.

The hundred miles from Wyoming to Teaoga was covered in 12 days, with 8 stops—the longest at Wyalusing, where rain and the demands of nature, hunger and cleanliness, combined to detain them. Two days later, August 9th, having passed the dreaded Breakneck Narrows with a minimum of casualties, they reached the beautiful and extended plain of Sheshecunninck on the east bank, overlooked by the great wooded range to the west. Here, on the spot named 'Haven of Rest' by early Moravian voyagers, the officers relaxed in a brief *al fresco* repast before proceeding to camp at the Upper Narrows. A scouting party under Captain Franklin pushed on to spy out the Promised Land—Teaoga—from the trail above the Turn; while the army rested for a day, and the line of march underwent revision.

The next day after, the army forded the river to Esther's Flats (Greene's Landing), holding hands in platoons to prevent being swept away by the current. Cautiously they advanced up the flats under a blazing August sun, covered by cannon from the boats, lest the work of Hartley's men might not have been completed, or the evil genius of the place still lurk in her old haunts. Meeting no one, they forded again, the swifter waters of the Chemung, and with triumphant music detrained about one o'clock, August 11 at the rendezvous appointed. The second lap of the journey was over. They had reached Teaoga.

On the Point, the old Indian clearings (now Tioga Point Farm and a tempting field for aviators) offered ample acreage for pegging in the tents of an army, for corraling the great herd of cattle and tired pack-horses also. The rest of the peninsula with its dark mysterious growth of oak and butternut and evergreen (uncleared except for Secord's seven acres and the old council-ground at the Neck) might easily conceal an ambushed enemy. Accordingly the fleet of boats and sun-burnt oarsmen advanced up the rivers to guard the portage—Butler's and Brant's favorite crosscut. The Light Corps under General Hand, versed in Indian tactics by his service at Fort Pitt,[20] made their way along the shore, encountering no enemy.

[20] Where he was unfairly branded for his "Squaws' Campaign."

Joined by Proctor's artillery, they took up position in the clearing from river to river (a 190-yard line), effectively blocking the passage of any war party.

That same night scouts led by Lieut. John Jenkins (later surveyor of the Point for Connecticut) reported activity at the 30-cabin Indian village of Chemung, 10 miles above. After a day's rest, therefore, and an eloquent address from their Commander, a large part of the army pushed on at night, only to find at dawn the town abandoned and the enemy in retreat. In a short pursuit and skirmish ensuing, the casualties were 7 killed and 11 wounded, after which the troops turned back to burn the cabins and destroy the crops—a heavy task, for the soil was rich on these lovely flats, and with Tory help not only corn but beans, potatoes, tobacco and turnips had been planted. Corn was to be the principal item on the soldiers' diet, when they marched north two weeks later on half rations.

"Returned at Night to Tioga much Fatigued," runs the diary of Lieut. Gore—who was to live to play a prominent rôle in the development of the valley.[21] After burying their seven dead with military honors near the Fort,

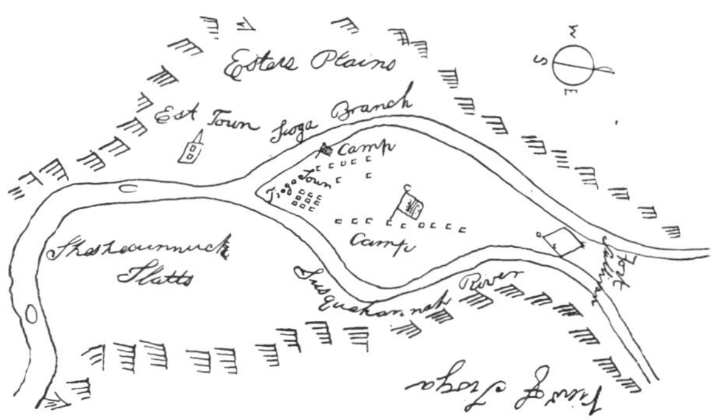

NUKERCK'S SKETCH OF SULLIVAN'S ENCAMPMENT 1779

as a granite marker now informs us, the Army set to work next day in earnest. Tents must be cut up by awkward fingers and stitched into bags, for flour could not be carried across country in barrels. At the Neck, a fort must be erected to serve as storage base for supplies and ammunition, and as hospital for the sick and wounded when the army struck north into the Iroquois country.

Diamond-shaped, about 90 yards on a side, the stockade stretched from river to river across the old Carry and clearing. A two-story blockhouse with mounted cannon guarded each angle.[22] Trees were felled and 12-foot logs set upright in a trench, palisade-fashion. An abattis of logs with pointed ends and a tangle of branches was laid outside to impede enemy approach—though no enemy seems ever to have essayed it.

Just where did the old fort stand, and are any vestiges of it visible today? The northern angle was probably on Secord's clearing, below the

---

[21] Eulogized in verse by Alexander Wilson, the Scotch ornithologist, for the hospitality extended him on his trip up the Susquehanna in 1804.

[22] The east and west corners are indicated today by low markers, the *Carry* by a tablet set in the Tioga St. bridge across the Chemung.

Museum site and not far from the Sullivan boulder on present Perkins property (721 S. Main St.). The late E. H. Perkins (died 1902) recalled the line of the southern earthwork below his brother's property (729 S. Main), clearly discernible a hundred years ago. An old timbered pit where ammunition was probably stored was discovered when excavating for a main to the Tannery about 1880. The Indian burial-ground located in 1882-3 on M. P. Murray's property (735 S. Main) may be the one soldiers were prohibited from disturbing, according to Colonel Barber's Order Book, 'lest our Oneida, Tuscarora and Stockbridge guides take offence.' The heading 'Fort Sullivan,' though Chaplain Rogers records its adoption on August 16,[23] was first used in the Order Book August 23.

Hardly a day passed at Teaoga without some evidence of the presence all about of lurking Indians. August 15th a boy in a party pasturing cattle on the open flats west of the Chemung was caught and scalped. His companions pursued the marauders up the western ridge and over Round Top—a long fruitless chase luckily with no further casualties.[24] All night alarms were likely to go popping off due mainly to the nervousness of sentries (possibly with the idea of promoting wakefulness, since the penalty for sleeping at one's post was 50 to 100 lashes.) Many raw recruits, indeed, in spite of six weeks drill at Wyoming, appear to have behaved like schoolboys, drawing out strict orders against the reckless firing of muskets at all hours, and the untimely practise of the Indian warwhoop. Restrictions against bathing "for fear of intermittent fever" appear to have been removed, however, and no one was sentenced to run the "gauntlope" in punishment.

August 16 a detachment of 900 under Generals Poor and Hand was despatched with 8 days' rations up the Susquehanna to meet Clinton's brigade, now anxiously awaited. Had he been ambushed by Thayendanegea (Joseph Brant), who claimed this segment of the river as his private warpath? Four days later, however, the young scout Lieut. Thomas Boyd (who was to meet a tragic fate within the month) returned with the welcome news that the forces had met without accident at Chukenut (near Owego).[25] Clinton had built 200 boats on Otsego, dammed the outlet until the flow (in midsummer only a thread) was sufficient to support the boats. He then had the dam cut, and in the resultant 'fresh' floated his boats laden with men and cannon downstream.

On August 22 the escort sent by Sullivan, augmented by Clinton's force of 1500 returned in a drenching downpour; some in boats, others across country from Wappasening and down Litchfield hill under Indian guides. A boisterous salute of thirteen guns and spirited airs from the military band greeted them. The rest of the day was spent in hunting up friends in different regiments and exchanging news.

Preparations for the final leg of the journey into the Indian country was eagerly pushed forward. Axes, scythes and hatchets for carving a way through the undergrowth were sharpened, ammunition distributed, rations issued and cooked. Three Oneida guides arrived, but rain delayed the start. On the first day out (August 26) only four miles were covered, the army

---

[23] A fifteen-foot model of the whole stockade, part of which is now in the Museum, was made for the Sesquicentennial in 1929 by a local Scout troop.

[24] Two days later one of a party hunting strayed officers' horses was 'shott through the Boady with three Balls, afterwards speered, tomyhawked and skalped."

[25] Actually at a point known ever since as Union.

encamping near Spanish Hill—to discover next morning that the Chemung had risen three feet; fording was out of the question. These delays proved fortunate, however, for the Newtown ambuscade of desperate Tory and Indian under Brant and Butler, behind elaborately camouflaged earthworks, grew restive under two days of broiling sun, their green screen withered. The plan for ambushing the army and stampeding horses and cattle was foiled by careful scouting. Screaming shells and well-aimed cannon balls —coupled with sturdy action of foot-soldiers, in a flanking movement—broke the enemy's morale. The Indians fled in panic, and Sullivan's troops turned to the destruction of the 50 houses and 100 acres of planting, ripe for the harvest.

Boats and the heavier cannon were then sent back to the fort, prepara-

Sullivan Boulder

Marks north limit of fort. The ball was used in a small cannon carried by hand, known as the 'Grasshopper'.

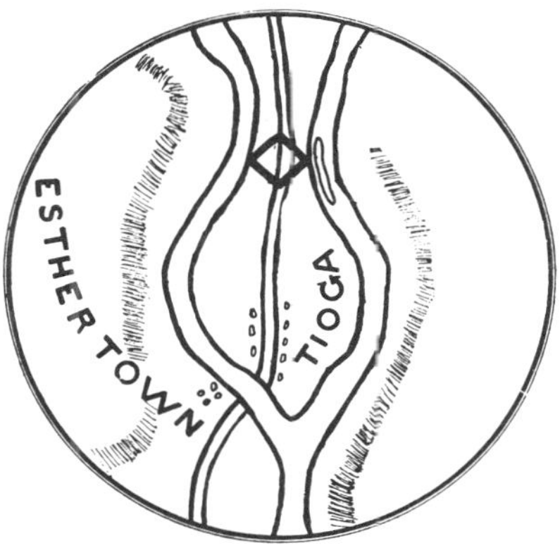

Sullivan's Route

tory for the plunge north into the wilderness.[26] Ploughing through a vast morass, and passing the deserted village of Esther's sister, Catherine Montour, the long troop-train pushed up the east shore of Seneca to destroy the extensive storage houses and harvest at Canadesaga (Geneva)—always to find the inhabitants in retreat before them! The fatal scouting error that cost Lieut. Boyd his life but spared the army a disastrous ambuscade, the arrival of the expedition September 14 at Genesee Castle, chief village of the Senecas, stronghold of Little Beard, and western door of the Long House, only to find its occupants departed, is a familiar tale.[27] Thousands of bushels of garnered corn, ears of which were declared twenty inches long,

---

[26] Wisely, since often 2-300 men were required to drag a cannon through a swamp.

[27] Graphically outlined in the journals of Lieutenants Hubley and Gore, fantastically sketched in Chambers' *Hidden Children*, and lately admirably retold in Elsie Singmaster's *R fles for Washington*.

were destroyed, 128 houses burned, and the Indians driven off toward Niagara.

The task set by Washington had been accomplished. Acres of orchards and gardens along a 125-mile track had been laid waste, and the weary forces could return, certain that the back of the Confederacy was broken. A lean winter faced the garrison at Niagara, crowded with hordes of starving savages. Last but not least, British generals had been kept guessing as to whether Canada or Virginia was Washington's next field of action.

Meanwhile at Fort Sullivan at the southern door of the Confederacy life had gone on not uneventfully, judging by the order book of Thomas Gee. Col. Israel Shreve with his little garrison of 300 had maintained guard over the flotilla of a half-thousand boats.[28] Mindful of the disaster at Fort Free-

Carry Marker Set in Chemung Bridge at Athens

Indicating portage where Indians carried their canoes across to ascend the other river.

lands fifty miles below in late July, and of the earlier fate of Forty Fort, painfully conscious of his isolation and shortage of provisions, Shreve issued the following eloquent appeal:

> Should this post be attacked, every person must be sensible there is no retreat, and to surrender to savages is worse than death. Spiritedly to defend the works, to conquer or bravely perish is the determined resolution of the commanding officer, and he has not the least doubt that every officer and soldier will stand by him to the last with undaunted bravery.

Perseverance in the completion of the works, through the sultry August weather, and meticulous care of firearms was enjoined on all. All women not needed as nurses or laundresses were urged to return in the boats going down for supplies, but many, even under threat of starvation, preferred the relative security of the stockade, and the shorter line of communication with relatives in the line of march. Supplies were presently received from below, and the wounded sent down from Newtown and Geneva despatched to Wyoming on crude litters strung across the boats. A temporary supply

---

[28] Chaplain Rogers declares 1200 were left in the fort, indicating there were 900 non-combatants—boatmen, women and children, along with the sick and wounded.

base for the returning troops was also erected near present Elmira by Colonel Reid, and named in his honor.[29]

On September 30 the victorious forces returned, marching in military order down the peninsula, saluted by cannonade and drum and fife. They had burned 41 villages and destroyed 200,000 bushels of corn, as well as quantities of fruit-trees, with a loss of only 41 men—though the diet of green corn necessary to supplement the half-rations carried had invalided many.

Two days after their return, General Sullivan "made an elegant entertainment for all the officers," ending up with an Indian dance (on the very spot where war-party after war-party had been launched against the settlements). The dance was led by an Oneida, and the officers, gay as boys, wore Indian masks, hopping about grotesquely in their tattered uniforms and punctuating the performance with warwhoops. Next day the supplies, the sick and wounded and *those without shoes* were loaded on the boats, and the expeditionary forces moved down the river. A fatigue party demolished the stockade and threw the logs in the river. Blockhouses, barracks and abattis were burned.[30] Sullivan's Expedition, along with Hartley's, had passed into history. Congress and the Commander-in-chief despatched their congratulations on its successful outcome. Mothers, wives and sweethearts heaved a momentary sigh of relief—though officers were required to report back at Easton without furlough.

The long Indian day of Teaoga was over.

---

[29] Here the returning army first went off their succotash diet, feasting on roast bullock. A salute of 13 guns was fired, and there were 13 candles and 13 toasts at the officers' party. Two of the toasts reveal the high spirits and Celtic wit of the party. One besought Providence to endow Congress and Legislature (whose laggard supplies had doubled the difficulties of the campaign) with all wisdom and virtue. Another ran "May all our enemies be mitamorphosed (sic) into packhorses, and sent on a western expedition against the Indians."

[30] Sometimes an uprooted tree today reveals a line of red ash on the old fort site.

III. PIONEER SETTLERS: PENNSYLVANIA-CONNECTICUT LAND FEUDS: 1786-1827

1786—a new chapter opens at Teaoga! Gone is the Indian, save for a few cabins on the Point, along the Chemung Narrows, and at Tutelo Creek; a few stragglers who return each season to lament over the graves of their forefathers, and barter furs, moccasins or snowshoes for powder, calico and copper kettles.[1] Gone is the Tory, except for Daniel Moore (turned patriot) at the old Ferry below the Island. Secord's pitch on the Indian camp and council-grounds has passed to a survivor of the Wyoming Massacre, Matthias Hollenback, for 100 pounds. Just south of the Museum site, near the old Tory well, this enterprising Astor of the Susquehanna has set up a trading-post, one of a chain reaching to Newtown, some say even to Niagara, serving alike Indian, white settler and government official en route for treaty grounds.

Gone is the Revolutionary army, 5000 strong, and brush is growing on the site of Sullivan's Fort. But peace has hardly settled on the Valley. Discord threatening the newly sealed brotherhood of the thirteen states has risen on our borders, and even old Benjamin Franklin, President of Pennsylvania, is shaken from his philosopic calm. The last campaign of the Yankee-Pennamite War launched at Wyoming in 1763 is about to be fought out in our township. For forty years it will absorb the attention of press, politicians and legislature, making and breaking candidates and parties as the lines of Federalist and anti-Federalist shift and reform into Republican and Democrat. The controversy will 'cost the State millions of dollars, and wear out a generation.' For every square foot of our lovely valley there will arise two claimants—sometimes three or more.[2]

With mingled pride and chagrin we approach this chapter in our annals. Let us set down the initial facts of the controversy warily, for the lines of the old feuds are etched deep, and the old fires still smoulder. Let us pass quickly over the old recriminations, the epithets of 'banditti' and 'land-jobber' hurled by opposing factions of our forefathers; the charges of assault and battery, arson, tar-and-feathering, and lesser peccadillos such as shaving the tail and mane of a rival surveyor's mount. If Western Pennsylvania, Massachusetts and the Hudson had their Whisky and Shay's rebellions, the South its Ku Klux, so we also our League of Wild Yankees

---

[1] Next year, however, they will return in force, to demand satisfaction for the murder of an Indian near Hollenback's, and to bury Captain Cornelius (Ka-nau-kawis), Onondaga chief, killed by his own people because he had 'gone white,' and planned to educate his son at a white man's college.

In 1790-91 they will gather again, 400 strong, on their old council grounds on the Neck (present Academy Green and Episcopal church sites—location on the old Fair Grounds is an error). Here they will hold a moonlight feast at the white man's expense, and bicker with Robert Morris' son over the sale of their old haunts northward. Rivalry between the Oneidas, our friendly guides in 1779, and the Cayugas, who sided with the King, will all but bring the ensuing dance to a bloody close—till an old chief knocks down the bragging-post and kicks out the fire. Later the women, bribed by the offer of hundreds of bushels of corn yearly, will cast the deciding vote, spelling the loss of the best of their New York lands (the Phelps-Gorham Purchase) to the white man. Thereafter a flood of immigrants will pour through old Teaoga, bound for the farmlands and orchards of the Finger Lakes.

[2] One of the peace-loving pioneer ancestors of the writer paid three times for his farm, buying first of the Susquehannah Company, later satisfying two Pennsylvania claimants.

in the period of our adolescence. This was both a frontier and a border colony. Few such have escaped a Cain-and-Abel period, and the over-zealous services of Vigilantes.

Decree of Trenton and Last Indian Purchase. Briefly, then, in 1782, before even a preliminary peace had been signed with England, a commission from seven states chosen by Congress to adjust the dispute over the overlapping royal charters met at Trenton. Unwilling to mar the newly sworn amity of the thirteen colonies, Connecticut gracefully withdrew her claims to jurisdiction over the territory covered by Penn's later charter. Whereupon, in

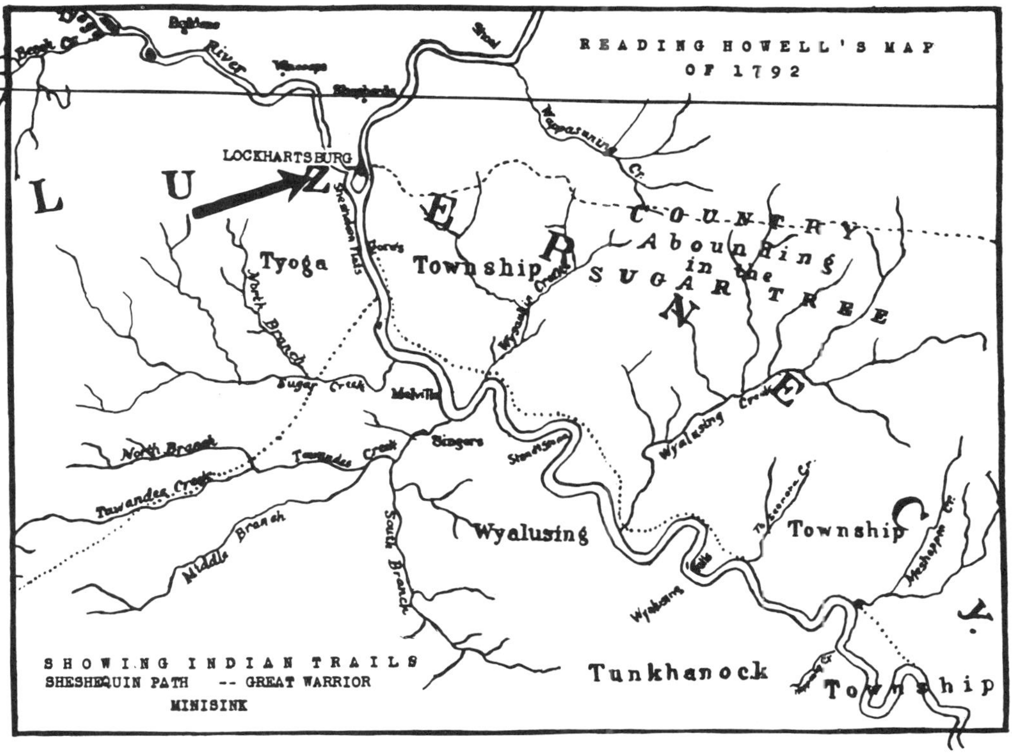

FROM READING HOWELL'S MAP OF 1792

Showing upper Luzerne County and Lockhartsburg named for the Pennsylvania purchaser of Tioga Point of 1798.

1784-5, our Commonwealth at Fort Stanwix prevailed upon the Indians to cede the last vestiges of their title within Penn's grant, running along below the 42nd parallel from the Chemung and Susquehanna to Ohio. This is known as the Last Purchase. The central portion, inclusive of our valley, was immediately absorbed into the great sprawling county of *Northumberland.*

The 'Indian Arrow' Patented to Lockhart. Next, Pennsylvania, in sore need of cash to pay Revolutionary debts and set on foot improvements, offered for sale in 1785 at Lancaster (our capital) land warrants for 400 to 1000 acres in the new lands along the hilly forested northern borders of the state. One Josiah Lockhart, local merchant, having paid 12 pounds

3 shillings (along with 704 other applicants) for a lottery ticket, drew number one, and acquired a thousand odd acres in our peninsula between the rivers, reaching from the Point up Mile Hill.[3] Promptly he despatched surveyors to the tract, patenting it next year under the appropriate title of *The Indian Arrow*. Maps of the period show the name *Lockhartsburgh* in the crotch between the rivers. *Trouble coming!* Teaoga, century-old capital of the Andastes, gateway of the Iroquois Long House, rendezvous of the Revolutionary Army, has passed into the hands of a Scotch-Irish shopkeeper of Lancaster.

During the same years, 1785-86, the Commonwealth sent out a party to run an accurate boundary line from the Delaware west along the New York border.[4] To forestall the claims of the Susquehannah Company, a new county, Luzerne, was next carved out of old Northumberland, with protective arms spread over present Bradford, Susquehanna, and adjacent territory, and county-seat at Wilkes Barre; and justices appointed.

Meanwhile, though abandoned by the mother state, Connecticut, Susquehannah Company subscribers back in Windham, along with others who had already migrated to Wyoming (said to have numbered in all 1200), were not idle. Having paid hard cash for their shares, they resolved to grip fast the rights conceded by the Royal Charter and the Indian deed, however fantastic in the light of modern geography and the demolished doctrine of the divine right of kings. Since the war, taxes ran high in New England (this was the year of Shay's Rebellion), families were voluminous, and the soil overworked. Agents extolled the marvelous richness and fertility of the Susquehanna valley.

The Susquehannah Company's Eighteenth Township—Athens. Certain landhungry shareholders, therefore, in 1786, just after Lockhart secured his patent, induced the Company to lay out an eighteenth township, five miles square, on the northern border of Westmoreland, as they called their western appanage. Hastily, on a Sunday morning, they ran a survey. Fifty-three town lots were plotted and assigned each to a proprietor, with a lot each reserved for school, church and minister. Ten to 100-acre farm-lots were also laid out to the north and south, and east and west of the rivers along the Indian flatlands. The township was defiantly christened with the name of the classical exemplar of democracy, Athens; and the aid of Ethan Allen invoked to erect a border state, independent both of Connecticut the betrayer, and of Pennsylvania the arrogant and greedy.[5] For this Col. John Franklin, our old Revolutionary scout, one of the three in whose name the township was launched, was held in a Philadelphia prison from 1788 to 1789, on the charge of high treason. Letters in cipher had been passed, and arms are said to have been stored hereabouts.

The Wild Yankees and Pickering's Abduction. Foreseeing trouble, the the Susquehannah Company had offered special terms to a number of 'Half-Share Men' (henceforth known as the Wild Yankees), sworn to de-

---

[3] Bounded on the west by 'Tioga creek' and located in Northumberland county. Copies of draught and patent and a letter from Josiah are filed in the Museum.

[4] An observatory for astronomical observations was located on Spanish Hill. The 59th milestone, set near Shepard's creek, and a latitude marker dated 1786 are in the Museum.

[5] Regarded as the last stronghold of tyranny and oppression, in part because of the old aristocratic manor-granting system of the Penns, in part because of alleged lobbying by Philadelphians.

fend their holdings for three years with their lives.[6] This and the growing resolve of the Pennsylvania Landowners (many of whom were men of means in Philadelphia)[7] to stand by their legal rights along the northern border naturally provoked complications. Following the arrest of Colonel Franklin, the Connecticut claimants abducted Colonel Timothy Pickering (Washington's trusted agent in this and Indian affairs, Revolutionary Quartermaster, later Secretary of War and State in Washington's cabinet). Pickering, who was stationed at Wilkes Barre during this stormy period, was held for a while by his abductors as a hostage for Franklin.

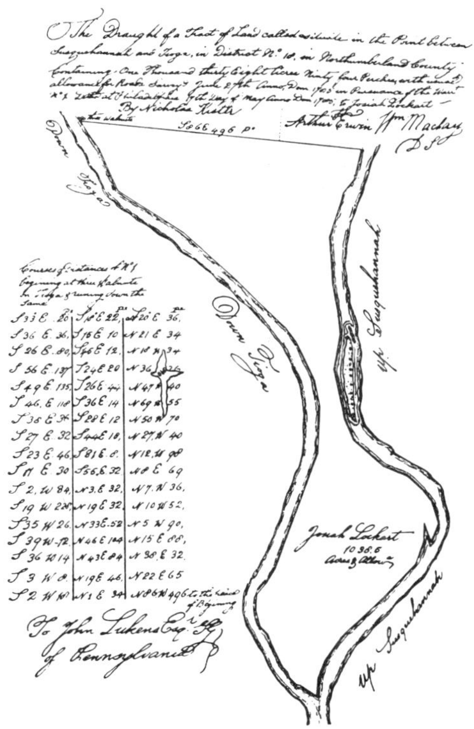

Surveyor's Sketch of Lockhart's Indian Arrow

Ringleaders and Irreconcilables along with Franklin at this period were Elisha Mathewson and Elisha Satterlee, who settled at Athens in 1788. Old settlers used to say that such was the fiery temperament of the latter that snow would not long lie on his grave, though the plump, placid features of his son, John Franklin Satterlee, in the portrait on the Museum

---

[6] Twice also in 1785-86 they shifted the boundaries of the seventeenth township Ulster, found to overlap the eighteenth. Legislative concessions usually covered only Ulster grants (prior to the decree of Trenton), hence confusion followed.

[7] Therefore able to send surveyors and agents to the spot, open roads, develop the country and perhaps influence legislation. They were able also to tap foreign markets; and in the uncertain years of the French Revolution and the Napoleonic wars (1789-1814) somewhat shabbily conveyed much of the northern border of Pennsylvania to French, Dutch, Swiss and Belgian individuals and companies. In this way, Madame de Stael, the famous French authoress, came into ownership of 4000 acres east of Athens—perhaps on the Windham hills.

walls, and the peaceable character of his descendants would seem to belie this verdict.[8]

Though balked of her high destiny as a Fourteenth State by the untoward incidents above related—and others—our little Township, along with her contemporary the Federal Constitution, worried along for a dozen years in relative calm. True, certain Acts of the Pennsylvania Assembly, the Confirming Law of 1787 (refusing to legalise Connecticut grants made after 1782, later repealed), and the Intrusion Act of 1795 (warning off later

Baltimore Purchaser of One-Third of 'Indian Arrow'

Connecticut claimants with threat of armed ejection), caused ripples of alarm, not allayed by certain lawless border happenings. For the original northern boundary, as surveyed hastily on a Sunday morning in 1786 by John Jenkins, just a month after the granting of Lockhart's Patent, ran south of Spanish Hill, along the earlier State Line of 1784-5. Many moved into the no-man's-land thus left below the new State Line of 1786 to avoid trouble. In vain, since this area also tempted certain lawless characters and fugitives from justice.[9] The township, furthermore, shortly ran its boundary and grants on up to the new line.

Sale of Lockhart's Patent to a Maryland-Connecticut Group. In 1798, however, the storm-clouds gathered in earnest. Relying on the protection of the Intrusion Act of 1795, Lockhart sold his 12-pound purchase for 6000 pounds to three mercantile partners of Baltimore. A lumber ark from

[8] Fifty pounds was offered for Elisha's arrest in 1784 when still a resident of Wyoming. His great-grandson C. Hyatt Satterlee was for many years an officer of Tioga Point Historical Society.

[9] The murder of Col. Arthur Erwin, prominent Pennsylvania claimant, occurred in this strip.

the Cohochton had just reached the Chesapeake, and these men forthwith envisaged the Susquehanna as the great waterway of the future, link between the Chesapeake and the Great Lakes. The names of the three were George and Ashbel Welles, Connecticut shipbuilders and sea-merchants, trading from Hartford to Baltimore, and Richard Caton, son-in-law of Charles Carroll of Carrollton.[10] Carroll, of an old Irish family, one of the signers of the Declaration of Independence, and later inaugurator of the Baltimore-Ohio Railroad, was an excellent business man, who already owned many large tracts in upper Pennsylvania, and eventually assumed much of the Lockhart purchase. Caton himself, English by birth, never resided here, though he came once in 1802 with his two daughters, famous beauties of the day, who later married into the British aristocracy. Dr. Hopkins is said to have been their host at Athens.

George Welles, Connecticut by birth and graduate of Yale, came on with his family in 1798-99 from Glastonbury, establishing a store on one corner of the Square, and building a thousand dollar wharf on the Susquehanna.[11] He began by buying up the titles of ten of the Connecticut claimants on Tioga Point below the village to the tune of about $2000, and contracting (with Caton) for the purchase from James Irwin of the Connecticut title for 14 town lots and 18 ten-acre lots, for $6000. Fearful of the operation of the Intrusion Act, all were apparently only too glad to dispose of contested titles—with one exception, Elisha Mathewson, Franklin's early associate and boon companion. Having acquired Connecticut rights to 125 acres located spottily about the farm, for 30 years he held out pertinaciously against all offers.

The perplexities of farming and harvesting an area dotted irregularly with the fields of an unfriendly neighbor, with annual floods carrying off fences and landmarks, are obvious; though in view of the threats of tar-and-feathering, arson and murder meted out to other Pennsylvania claimants, Welles may be accounted lucky. The wave of failures and bankruptcies throughout the States and Europe following in the wake of the Napoleonic wars crippled both his partners and himself. The blundering legislation of Pennsylvania seeking to do justice to both sets of land claimants added to the confusion.[12] The year after matters were brought to a partial head by an ejection warrant issued in Charles Carroll's name against Elizabeth Mathewson, widow of Elisha, Welles built his home on the west side of Main Street on his block of town lots in the Arrow; succumbing in 1813 to the mysterious 'cold plague.' Only after the death of both of the principals in this long controversy was it finally terminated by

---

[10] Described by Lockhart as 'the most hournourable Gentlemen—the Verry men to Settle all the trobles in that Country.' The original indenture or deed of 1798, Lockhart's letter, and copies of the fine Copley portraits of Caton and Carroll are in the Museum, along with facsimile of a sketch of George Welles in uniform leading a company of Yale students at the time of British raids along the Sound in 1777-81. The Welles brothers were descendants of Thomas Welles, one of the first proprietors and colonial governors of Connecticut.

[11] The town was laid out anew in 1802 with the aid of James Pumpelly of Owego, later George Welles' son-in-law. Two streets parallel with Main or Union were plotted along the rivers, there were a number of cross-streets named for Carroll, Caton, and Welles, and two Squares. Pumpelly's father had been one of Roger's Rangers, sole survivor in a scouting expedition to St. Francis.

[12] Throughout this period Pennsylvania endeavored by suitable legislation to find some legal solution involving as little hardship as possible to both parties. She was inclined, however, to draw the line at new grants made defiantly by the Connecticut Company after the Decree of Trenton (1782).

act of Legislature in 1827. With what results we shall see later. Meanwhile let us take a look at the expanding village at the beginning of the new century.

George Welles: Early Pennsylvania Proprietor
Leading a company of Yale students against British during Revolution

Old Tioga Point in 1800

Tavern and Trading-Post. No mere internal dissension, however bloody, could hold Tioga Point back from her destiny. Southern doorway in the past to the Iroquois Confederacy, she was now turnstile to the Promised

Land of the Revolutionary soldier. Thousands were returning along the routes carved by Sullivan's axemen, to take possession of the new lands opened up in western New York State by foreign capital.[13]

Thirty Conestoga wagons a night were sometimes drawn up at the Square, around which sprang up inns and shops. At the southeast corner rose Mathewson's Red Tavern (Loveland's, 717 S. Main today); at the northeast corner, Irwin's shop and inn (Page's and Keefe's, 711 and 713). Hollenback's two-story log trading-post on the southwest corner (Hunsiker's, 728 S. Main) carried a tavern license also. At Ferry street (now Tioga), at the entrance of the village, was Saltmarsh's Public (742, still standing though altered), prepared to lodge strangers overnight, or provide stagecoach passengers with breakfast; as was also Alexander's opposite.

In 1790 when Col. Eleazer Lindley (veteran of Sullivan's Expedition) came through from Morristown, N. J., transporting his colony of sixty up the river by boat and horse, the resources of the infant hamlet were stretched to the limit. Perhaps the caravan tented on the Green. And if the Susquehannah Company, hundreds strong, actually met here as reported in 1795, they can only have followed suit; as must also the 400 Indians who gathered for the treaty council in 1790-91 (said to have met on the present Episcopal church site, now narrowed by flood erosion).

For at the opening of the century the hamlet at the Neck was little more than a 25-acre slashing in the forest, with a dozen or so frame houses, and possibly a few log shacks. In 1795 the Duke de Liancourt had reported eight or ten dwellings only. On either side the long street now South Main, probably hacked out by Sullivan's men in 1779, lay the 53 lots plotted by the Connecticut company, though the town plot probably was as yet only partly cleared. From Burying Ground Hill, beginning just above the present Presbyterian church, the numbers ran down the west side of the street 1-26 (now Dana Macafee's, 756). Crossing over, the numbers 27 to 53 ran up the east side (to present Clovercroft, 615). Fifty families was regarded as the ideal size for a town group.

About four doors above the Museum site, David and Clement Paine, from Cape Cod, the former secretary for the Susquehannah Company and later our first Burgess, had a pleasant two-winged cottage surrounded by trees and shrubbery (burned 1870). Both were active in promoting civic enterprises, having come with high hopes of starting a newspaper. Across the street and higher up, on the site of the present Episcopal rectory, Dr. Stephen Hopkins, David's brother-in-law, who had dropped off from Colonel Lindley's party, was soon to build a yet more pretentious and hospitable residence (serving at times as an inn), to replace his earlier home of 1795 below the Red Tavern, (said to have been the first frame dwelling in Athens).[14] Here at 'the Doctor's Hotle' a 'fandango with 30 or 40 couples' and an 'evening of social glee' are reported about 1802 by one of the Paines, indefatigable letter writers, to whom we are indebted for a large share of our knowledge of these early years.

The doctor himself, a gentleman of the old school, is recalled for his tireless service over miles of countryside from Wilkes Barre to Palmyra,

---

[13] The estate of the British Pulteneys in the Bath and Geneva district (present Steuben and Ontario counties); and the Holland Land Company holdings westward on the Genesee (Allegany, Cattaraugus and Genesee counties).

[14] This new house had a famous upper bow window facing the street. The two wings which were later moved off and converted into separate dwellings may perhaps be located on Hopkins Street today.

his record of attendance at 2500 births and his benevolent burning of all bills when he felt death close upon him. His daughter was to become the wife of Lawyer Edward Herrick (afterward judge), accompanying her husband to Ohio on horseback on her bridal tour. Her portrait in white satin and corkscrew curls, believed to have been painted by one of her family, is in the Museum, though she is best remembered by the sprightly silhouette, taken at the same time as her husband's dignified profile.

Opposite the Saltmarsh Tavern, on what is now Maurice property, a Scotchman of enterprise and varied talents presided over a miniature patriarchal community, with residence, inn, horse gristmill, distillery, wharf and log schoolhouse. Here he lived for twenty years, inaugurating many ventures in real estate and industry, and rearing a family of ten children; later moving West, to set the pace in a new community.[15] In the tax-list of 1796 of Tioga Township (the Pennsylvania election district

David and Clement Paine

Who promoted the interests of the Susquehanna Company at Tioga Point

covering our area) Alexander's assessment is $1324—an amount only equalled or surpassed by 9 men in an area reaching from Sheshequin to Milltown.

From this tax-list, containing 163 names, and that of 1808 (both printed in O.T.P., 682 f.), along with the clientele recorded in the old account books of Hollenback's and Caton and Welles' may be culled the names of the Valley's first 'four hundred.' The residences of the eighteen whose valuation runs over $1000, indicating in that day that they were men of enterprise and ability, will carry us up to Milltown (John Shepard's), across to Tutelo (Toodley) Town (Daniel McDuffee's), down to Greene's Eddy (Wright Loomis' and John Spalding's), to Ulster (Solomon Tracy's), across to Sheshequin (Obadiah Gore's and Joseph Kinney's), and to East Athens (John Franklin's and Elisha Satterlees's). Since the branches of the family trees in these outlying settlements are interwoven with our own in an intricate Persian pattern, we shall have to make use of the four or five Athens fords and ferries across the Chemung and Susquehanna: at Saltmarsh's, and probably near present Tozer's bridge, at Satterlee's (opposite the present Athens High School), and at Moore's or Northrup's (below the Island); as well as the five wharves (Irwin's, Mathewson's, Hollenback's, Alexander's and Welles') if we are to tell the story of the valley adequately. For this was preëminently a river town in the early eighteen hundreds.

Returning to the village rising around the Square (where there was in early days a cross-street) we may note the skeleton framework of the Academy to be, a 42x24 foot structure. This was raised shortly after the meeting in 1797, at which 26 townsmen subscribed $30 each toward an institution of learning such as they had known at Plainsfield, Connecticut.

[15] One of his grandaughters became Thomas Edison's wife.

It was to wait seventeen years, however, for completion,—until the early days of conflict were over, log-cabin schoolrooms must suffice, and religious and masonic gatherings be confined to private dwellings. Loghouses (with pegs set in alternate walls at a corner in lieu of stairs, beds whose footboard was a single post in the puncheon floor and oiled paper windows) doubtless still sufficed for many of the 'rude forefathers of the hamlet.' There was the cabin of Jared Root the schoolmaster above the Presbyterian church site, west of which lived William Prentice the postmaster, son of the druggist-doctor of Milltown who built Elm Cottage, cousin of John Shepard, and an early victim of one of the local epidemics. Hendy, pioneer of Elmira, had a shack on the Clovercroft site; Julius Tozer was probably in his early log-house on Susquehanna Cove.

Half the population are shop and inn-keepers, the remainder lumberers and farmers, with a mere peppering of doctors, lawyers, preachers and schoolteachers. Many combine several of these rôles in one person. Some of the minor crafts are represented. At the Point there is a rope-maker, supplying cords for the old cord beds; at the Neck a blacksmith, John Redington, shoeing horses and oxen. The McDuffees and McKinneys are skilled Scotch-Irish weavers (see the checked silk coat and the samples of blue and white coverlets in the Museum exhibits); and flax and hemp are allotted their due space in the fields. Carpenters and joiners are on the 1796 Tioga tax-list, though Justice Noah Murray sent back to Connecticut for his spacious cherry desk of many drawers and compartments when appointed in 1788. The Snells, early settlers in West Athens, are said to have been makers of beaver hats, bringing $5 apiece, though the Sunday head-dress of John Spalding, preserved in the museum (black beaver mounted on thin layers of wood) carries the trademark 'Christy's Best, London.'

Judge Herrick and His Wife Celestia Hopkins

In John Shepard's patriarchal little colony on Shepard or Cayuta Creek (Milltown) there is a German deerskin dresser (Snechenberger), making mittens, moccasins and breeches; a tanner, a shoemaker, a clothier, and a skilled carpenter, Dan Elwell, architect for the Paines' pleasant cottage at Athens, and possibly also for more than one of the dignified old frame dwellings of the period, with their long gables, ample end-chimneys (guarantee of a warm welcome within) and hospitable doorways with fan and sidelight.[16]

Local and home products are amply supplemented by goods brought up the river on 60-foot Durham boats or by sleds on the ice from Wyoming to Hollenback's; from Baltimore, or by wagon overland from Catskill on the Hudson, to Welles and Caton's or Irwin's.

Hollenback's trading-post at Tioga since 1783 had furnished supplies for the early surveying parties, Maclay's and others, and for Simon Spalding's pioneer Sheshequin group. Through the hands of his efficient agents, Shepard, Maxwell or Tuttle, had passed many of the goods for the Fort Stanwix treaty with the Indians, as well as Pickering's supplies for the councils at Teaoga and Painted Post in 1790-91. Through the Conyinghams in Wilkes Barre and Philadelphia, Hollenback doubtless had access to foreign markets, for witness the variety of goods available to the housewife as early as 1787. Broadcloth, flannel, calico, linen, muslin and corduroy were on his pricelists. Blankets, shawls, hose, hats, handkerchiefs, shoes, and shoebuckles were moderately priced. None need go without combs, needles and pins, scissors, razors and saws. There were teacups and saucers, tea, chocolate, sugar, cheese, snuff and soap for the fastidious. Almanacs, bibles, spelling and psalm-books and testaments could be purchased, along with a number of other commodities, such as ink-powder, and silver brooches and beads for the Indians.

Furs and wheat from the Genesee and Lake country were acceptable mediums of exchange, though Spanish milled dollars and guineas were not flouted, and bundles of shingles (cut surreptitiously in anyone's woodlot) were also current.

No household relied entirely on the trader, however. In every home there were moulds for dipping tallow candles; small flax wheels and reels where house-wives sat patiently at the treadle, turning the hatchelled strands into linen thread; larger wheels where girls stepped briskly back and forth twisting white masses of wool sheared from their own sheep into yarn; and, in the 'weave-room,' looms where clever fingers turned out patterned towels and table-linens, stout cloth for under and outer garments, the inimitable fine blankets of our grandmothers, or sometimes the elaborately checkered blue and white coverlets so prized today (see Museum exhibits). No one was idle.

Farming and Lumbering. In the outlying areas of the township, these were the main activities, with potash kilns and stills to care for the by-products of lumbering and the surplus corn. Every creek had at least one sawmill and some a half dozen Logs were brought down from the hills on sleds in winter, sliced up by a bucket-wheel fed from a sluice and geared to a saw making one downward cut to each revolution. The lumber was fastened together in huge rafts or 'arks,' and floated downstream in spring freshets, to be broken up for market—a hazardous, hair-raising adventure, owing to the many twists of the river, and precipitous ice-carved rocky narrows.

In East Athens, farming the fertile Indian flats, were Elisha Satterlee and John Franklin, McKinneys, Flowers and a number of others, mostly Connecticut claimants. Franklin's sturdy frame house on the upper terrace, begun in 1797 after his second marriage, to the widow Bidlack, is still occupied by a descendant, N. F. Walker. West of the Chemung was the log house of Jacob Snell, who had poled his family up the river in 1784,

---

[16] To saw- and gristmills were soon added fulling and woolen mills, in the angle between the creek and the river—hence *Milltown.*

and is reputed Athens' first permanent settler.[17] The fine bronze monument on the old Academy site, showing a soldier-pioneer and a boy drummer, with the inscription, *Pro Patria et Gloria,* was erected by his descendants. Farther down in West Athens, below the line of the old Carry, was the log house of Rev. Noah Murray, appointed justice in 1788 by the Governor to assist in allaying border troubles: and that of Capt. Joseph Spalding, grandfather of Jesse, donor of the Museum-Library. Morley's and Greene's would follow within the decade (where now are located the Thurston farm, Morley's mill and Greene's Landing).

MONUMENT TO DEFENDERS OF OUR COUNTRY
Erected in 1900 by descendants of first permanent settler Jacob Snell.

Where Tutelo creek enters the Chemung, another group, Tozers and McDuffees, was forming. The frame house of Ira Stephens built about 1800, with its third story ballroom, is still standing south of Spanish Hill. A spy-glass said to have been used by George Washington and presented by him to Ira, for Revolutionary service rendered, is in the Museum. Ira was a victim of border land feuds, murdered at Angelica in 1803. Alpheus Harris, whose family were Susquehannah Company claimants on the Point, will soon locate on a 400-acre tract at Spanish Hill—presently to be wrested from him by a Pennsylvania claimant. Eastward, on the Susquehanna, on the state line Adam Cranse was establishing a ferry and shad-

[17] From the Snells we have a vivid picture of the gathering of the Indians in 1790, braves and squaws in birchbark canoes, many in white blankets, with innumerable tinkling silver ornaments. Two typical hammered silver Iroquois brooches are in the Museum, bearing various curious symbols.

fishery. The Cranses were to become partners of John Shepard, who after 15 years' experience with Connecticut titles was about to invest in the 5000-acre Howell tract, carrying a Pennsylvania patent.

Twenty-five Years' Progress at Tioga Point

In the period between 1800 and the final settlement in 1827 of the Connecticut controversy by Legislature, the Valley passed through many vicissitudes, but made long strides forward. The dreaded war-whoop no longer rang through the forest, but fire, flood, disease and wild beast took their toll. Two mysterious epidemics in 1803-4 and 1813-14, known as the Cold Plague and the Sheshequin fever, yielding to no known remedies, carried off numbers of citizens. In the outlying districts in the absence of their husbands women armed with pitchforks chased bears, wolves, wildcats from the cattle-pens. During long hard winters, packs of wolves ranged through the pine forest where Sayre has now expanded, striking terror to the hearts of the mothers of small children. An army of locusts appeared, and devoured the foliage of trees and crops; returning again after fourteen years. At a community flax-hatchelling in the hills, a spark fired the floating particles in a low-ceiled room into combustion, like a gas explosion, fatally burning a mother and infant. Perennially, the flooded rivers took their toll of human victims, though there was no recurrence of the great 'Pumpkin Flood' of 1786. Men were struck by lightning bolts, thrown from their horses, caught between the stones of their gristmills. But village life went on.

While our infant government wrestled with the political problems raised by the bloody course of the French Revolution, and evolved the policy of no entangling alliances; and while our statesmen struggled to stabilize economics, in the wake of the world-wide financial chaos of the Napoleonic era, we in our remote valley were rocked also by world events, in the main stimulated to fresh endeavor. The refuge granted to French royalists 30 miles below us on the Susquehanna (with Matthias Hollenback's sage aid) raised the standards of shop and inn keepers, as well as the general level of living; bringing distinguished travellers through the Valley with new ideas and insistence on better roads and postal service. The Napoleonic wars drove European capital to invest in northern Pennsylvania and southern New York lands. Surveys, roads, land offices and often schools and churches were financed by these foreign syndicates, setting the section fifty to a hundred years ahead. Border disputes and unfriendly courts, however, often robbed the foreign owner of his just profit, the local settler being the chief gainer.

Next came the War of 1812, in which numbers from our township enlisted. In 1814, Captain Julius Tozer, who as a lad in his teens served in a Revolutionary drum-and-fife corps, recruited a company largely from his own relations. New England sea-captains who had lived by trade with the West Indies migrated to find new means of livelihood. With the embargo on our ports new sources of supplies must be found, new roads developed.

Roads already ran along the old Indian trails up and down the rivers—south to Wysauking (where John Shepard was part owner of the Connecticut township of Claverack, extending west along Towanda Creek), and on to Wilkes Barre. Up this dusty road, its mud-holes patched with corduroy, jostled by its ruts, all but hanging on one wheel in its narrows, must have travelled in the first quarter of the century Mrs. Jerome Bonaparte (Betsy Patterson of Baltimore) with her small son, coming in coach-

and-four with outriders in the style exacted by her imperial brother-in-law, to visit a friend, Mrs. Abner Murray of West Athens, and possibly other acquaintances in this vicinity. The Misses Caton may have travelled in the same fashion; but Joseph Bonaparte, ex-king of Spain, en route to his hunting-lodge in northern New York, probably came on horseback as did La Rochefoucauld, Maulevrier, Talleyrand, and other Frenchmen before him.

Le Ray de Chaumont, son of the French manufacturer who befriended us in the Revolution and owner of an 80,000-acre strip between Athens and the Delaware, journeyed by stage when he came from Leraysville, Jefferson County, to confer with his land agent Joseph Kingsbury at Sheshequin, first inquiring solicitously as to the number of 'narrows' along the highway. For there were post-routes to Newtown, Owego and across the Catskill foothills to the Hudson, headed toward the old Windham homeland in Connecticut. The Genesee Road from the West Branch, main highway of migrants to New York State, ran through the valley; though the later Berwick pike merely skirted the township on the west. Now, however, in 1812, a new route to the Finger Lakes was needed, to transport gypsum and salt, and the Cayuga and Susquehanna Turnpike Company was organized. The road to Ithaca was improved, and a tollgate located near Spring's Corners (Milltown), where an inn sprang up to accommodate stage passengers. Earlier this road had been so rough that the wagon bringing glass for Abner Murray's new house in 1807 upset, shattering much of the load.

During this period Bradford County (earlier Ontario) was cut off from the old mother county Luzerne (1812-14). Athens had been designed by some of the early fathers as a future countyseat, but the discovery of Barclay coal, and its more central position shunted the prize to Meansville (now Towanda). Our valley, however, had the honor of furnishing the first prothonotary, clerk, etc. (appointed by the Governor) Charles Fisher Welles, son of George, the first Pennsylvania claimant at the Point.

Education, Religion and Recreation

While completion of the Academy hung fire for seventeen years, education was not neglected. Leading settlers, among whom was more than one graduate of Yale and of various New England academies, saw to it that discipline and the three R's were within reach of all.[18] The Eighteenth Township was soon playing a prominent rôle in Legislature, and in 1814 a representative from our new county secured an appropriation of $2000 for the equipment and launching of the Athens Academy, and engaged a teacher, Sylvanus Guernsey, in Harrisburg. The colonnaded portals of the institution opened, and the classical dignity of Athens was complete, with instruction in the ancient languages, and in such Platonic branches as astronomy and higher mathematics.[19]

In spite of certain slanderous traditions current[20] and the fact that no

[18] At Milltown, Toodleytown, Greene's Eddy and Franklin's and either at Alexander's or on the northern edge of the Athens Townplot there were log schoolrooms, usually with male teachers.

[19] Along with such practical and unplatonic applications as the rudiments of surveying, invaluable to the pioneer.

[20] Due possibly to the existence in the valley of six stills, the pioneer's main reliance for ready money. Whisky was the specific for all ills, in the days antedating doctors and druggists, and appears regularly on the accounts of all early settlers in Gore's, Hollenback's and Welles' store books (many of them in the Museum).

'meeting-house' proper was erected before 1825, Hollenback's trading-lists and numerous well-worn family bibles indicate that the community was far from abandoning the religious predelictions of their New England ancestors. The reverend gentleman commissioned justice by the Commonwealth to promote peace among them had, however, advanced too far in the direction of pacificism to suit many. Abandoning the sterner dogmas of his native Connecticut, in the freer air of Penn's Woods he was preaching a gospel of universal peace. In this era of fierce feuds and deadly enmities, however, many of his fellow-townsmen felt the need of a place of eternal punishment to which to consign the erring. Shortly after the death of the gentle pacifist (in 1811), a travelling minister (Rev. William Wisner), stopping over the week-end to rest his lame horse, undertook to convince his hearers in a single discourse of 'the total depravity of the human heart.' With eminent success! He was invited to remain as pastor at $220 a year (supplemented by funds from *a Connecticut missionary society*), and for five years labored at 'Satan's seat, among Universalists and infidels.'[21]

An era of evangelism and repentance ensued, and Clement Paine's wife was moved to carry the gospel to the Indians of Georgia—returning with vivid impressions of the evils of slavery, antedating those of Fanny Kemble and Harriet Beecher Stowe.[22]

In the intervals of perennial worry over boundaries and titles, with the prospect of being driven overnight to abandon your cherished clearing and improvements to an earlier claimant, or pay double or triple to clear your title, recreation and amusement of various sorts was imperative. There were singing-schools and dancing (reels and quadrilles)—for all the more pretentious frame dwellings had third-story ballrooms.[23] Apart from the communal husking, quilting and 'raising' bees, there were the great ring hunts, sometimes bringing down 30 deer, winding up with barbecue suppers at an inn. There were joint shad fisheries too, in season, with great seines stretched across the river by parties in boats, and gleaming piles of fish heaped on the sandy coves of islands.[24] Some say there was horse-racing, also, to the scandal of the godly.

Athens Village in 1827

Before returning to the seething Susquehannah Company controversy' let us take a flying trip down Main Street, inspecting the changes wrought by a quarter-century, and noting the patchwork of Yankee and Pennamite residents. The little hamlet is now no mean replica of the neat white New England villages deserted by our ancestors some fifty or seventy-five years earlier, to seek their fortunes in the 'West.' In the central square, where militia drill weekly, rises the white porticoed Academy, its upper story a community hall for Masonic and various other gatherings—religious and civic. On the northwest border of the town plot, in the long shadow of the western ridge, rises the Presbyterian meeting-house, steepled or at least belfried. Opposite, behind its 'splint fence,' which sighs mournfully in the wind like a departed spirit, stand the Old Burying Ground (gift of Richard Caton), where already a number of 'the rude forefathers of the hamlet'—or their frailer children—sleep, under grey slabs carved with urn and laurel

[21] A number of denominations who were later to erect churches here maintained circuit-riding missionaries in this area throughout this period.

[22] See J. A. Perkins, *Early Times on the Susquehanna*, 1870, 200 f.

[23] Some curious old invitations survive, one asking a young lady and escort to an Independence Ball, at *three P.M. precisely*. Adding to its interest is the fact that the young lady was the justice-of-peace's daughter, the ball given by a prominent Connecticut claimant, July 3, 1808—the day preceding the serving of a famous ejection warrant.

[24] By 1825, with the building of dams, these were already passing.

by some unknown mortuary artist (note especially that of Ferdinand McDuffee, the 'Beau Brummel' of early Athens).

Around the Square, inns and shops still cluster. With the settlement of New York State, however, and the migration westward of the Indian, the fur trade has declined and shops have sprung up in all the nearby river towns. The embattled farmer, moreover, has already risen against the merchant, demanding a $1 credit for a 50-cent bushel of wheat. Hollenback, whose end approaches (he died in 1829 at his Wilkes Barre residence), no longer maintains an agent at the old historic loghouse, whose display windows have fallen into the hands of *milliners*. A new and spacious inn, Briggs' Tavern, colonnaded, surmounted by a 'captain's walk' and 'rather far uptown,' has risen (on Haverly's present site, 638 S. Main). This will later become famous as the Exchange Hotel, a north Pennsylvania stage-stop, for sixty years the vital center of the community.

Poplars, locusts and spruces, introduced by those two indefatigable town-builders, the Paines, shade the main residence street along the ridge of the peninsula. A dozen frame houses, mostly variants of the sedate long-gable design introduced by the Paine's architect, Dan Elwell, rise on either side. Many have wings at right and left for business, for not a townsman but is shop or inn-keeper in his spare moments. Hardly a dozen of these old-timers with their quaint small-paned (12 over 8) windows have survived fire and change in the village proper, though a number of contemporaneous dwellings can be located beyond the limits.

Above Briggs' Tavern, on a lot once assigned to Ethan Allen, stands the home of Dr. William Kiff, physician of Irish descent, waylaid here en route to Virginia.[25] Farther south is the old homestead of George Welles, Pennsylvania claimant with Carroll and Caton, and proprietor of the Point Farm, who was carried off by the epidemic of 1813. His eldest son, Henry, busy fighting out the claim in Legislature and hoping for a favorable outcome, has built a new stone house far down on the contested acres of the Point Farm. Henry's son-in-law, E. H. Perkins, of a Norwich Connecticut family, later consul at Santa Cruz in the Virgin Islands, will occupy for many years the old homestead (from 1833 on). Its quaint low-ceiled, panelled rooms, its spacious chimney-nooks and brass-knobbed latches are still remembered by the older generation. Opposite, on the Ahbe-Brennan site, David Cook, Henry Welles' cousin by marriage, later editor of the *Elmira Republican*, has built a commodious dwelling, 'embracing all the modern improvements and finished with Venetian blinds' (1818).[26]

Going still farther south, past Clement Paine's we find the home of the youthful Judge Herrick (another son-in-law of Dr. Hopkins), to become famous in later years as the boarding-place of Stephen Foster while a student at the Athens Academy. The Judge, however, has moved to a new residence on the banks of the Susquehanna, built by a Pennsylvania land agent, Michael Tharp. North of the village plot it stands, approached by a winding drive through spacious grounds long known as 'Herrick's Meadow', full of brush and red deer in the sixties, of buttercups and grazing cattle in the eighties.[27]

---

[25] A remarkable sampler produced at the age of eleven by Jane Walker of Ulster whom he married is preserved at the Museum, along with some of his early equipment.

[26] This house is still standing, moved to Hopkins St. when Henry's nephew Charles F. Welles, Jr. and his partner Chauncey Shipman requisitioned the site for their substantial residences and the Canal Company offices.

[27] The house, nicknamed the *Glass Palace* because of its long French windows, still stands, though altered. The meadow is built up solid with small homes.

Dr. Hopkins still dominates the village from his new hearthstone. His brother-in-law Ebenezer Backus, a postal agent, occupies his old home below the Red Tavern. South of this David Paine has transformed the old Alexander settlement to a residential estate, with shrubbery, trees, flower gardens and a new frame house, where the first village library will be opened, and where David's accomplished wife (from Portland, Maine) will give lessons in music and the higher branches to select pupils. The house has long since disappeared, replaced by a roomy modern mansion with well-kept lawns, flower-beds and fine old trees—still one of the beauty-spots of Athens.

The old ford and ferry over the Chemung (the Tioga Branch) was replaced in 1820 by a covered bridge with toll-gate. Ferry Street across the old Carry is closed and short Tioga opened. Justice Noah Murray, Jr. has located on the corner just south—to catch the horseback honeymooning couples who used to journey up to Squire Buck's at Chemung 'to be joined.' To the generation of loquacious ferrymen and stagecoach drivers will now be added a bevy of gazetteering toll-gate keepers, retailing all the gossip for miles up and down the river, and possibly detracting from our reputation for godliness by the violence of their oath-embroidered speech.

On the east side of Main, George A. Perkins, older brother of E. H., has a home (still standing) with druggist shop in the wing, to catch countrymen dashing over to town for first-aid remedies. In 1870 his wife will become the first historian of the valley, publishing a series of papers known as *Early Times on the Susquehanna.*

Across the river, Abner Murray has replaced his father's log-house with a long-gabled frame one (to function many years as an inn), with a huge chimneystack and six fireplaces, and a ball-room with folding seats and hinged partitions. Around the great fireplace and oven in the woodshed in the rear, teamsters and lumbermen reluctant to pay toll over to the village gather at night before roaring fires, to tell tall tales of their adventures along the river. Bunks along the wall are free to all.

Back in the village, an innovation, Brooks' hat factory, is just building on the Chemung bank on the southern edge of the plot—a site originally allotted to Nathan Denison (colonel in charge of the ill-fated Wyoming Forty-Fort in 1778). South Main St. boasts a private school also, kept by the Misses Robb, in a house still standing but altered. Built on the Susquehanna by a Pennsylvania land agent, Thomas Overton, it was later the residence of Dr. Thomas Huston, Hopkins' son-in-law.[28] Below on the Chemung stands the house of Lawyer Horace Williston (later Judge). This follows a new design, veering toward the neo-classic, with columns flattened to pilasters on its façade, and triangular pediment above—though the two wings for business offices are retained (now altered). South of the village plot, Rev. Wisner's son has built a log-house, last outpost against Satan.

North of the village plot a Welsh group, Davies, Parry and Jones, have bought a block of land of Henry Welles, also a number of the lots set apart for school revenues. Davies will presently build a residence far up town (where the Stimson House stood later). When the Susquehanna bridge is opened Davies will move this house back, enlarge it, and open it as the

[28] Dr. Huston's son-in-law, O. H. Worden, will edit the first local paper, the *Athens Scribe* (1841-2), his son Charles the *Athens Gleaner* (1870-74), gathering up much early history in their columns. Full files of these valuable old sheets have been deposited in the Museum by the editor and his descendants.

Coffee House—first temperance establishment on the Point.[29] The dignified white-pillared Elsbree house nearby was built by Davies' son-in-law, H. C. Phelps.

Farther up, in the suburbs, Clement Paine is developing Painesville between Paine St. and the present railway tracks. Farther still, on the Plains where Sidney Hayden will discover glacial clay beds and start a brick manufactory, Ashbel Welles' son has established residence.

On the cross-road between Milltown and Spanish Hill, not far from his uncle Alpheus Harris's claim, Harris Murray, grandson of Noah, has a log-house which will be replaced later by the fine old stone mansion still occupied by a descendant, John Harris Murray, Jr. In the upper reaches of the Township, John Shepard, after providing his group of craftsmen with a row of dwellings, and presenting the community with land for Rest Cemetery, has built himself a commodious new home farther east on the Susquehanna river, facing the island and Cranse's shad fishery. For many years the home of his daughter Mary (Mrs. Silas Fordham), it is still standing, though isolated by the shifting of population with railroad development.

For the rivers are no longer the valley highways. The wharves are falling to decay. In 1826, a 60-foot steamer, the Codorus, built at York, made her way upstream, visiting Williamsport, Binghamton and Elmira—a three months' cruise. The second steamer to attempt the journey, however, blew up on the rocks at Nescopeck, and the prospect of profitable river navigation waned. But the opening of the Erie Canal in 1826 revived the earlier project of transportation by canal. Athenians planned a line from Tioga Point to Cayuga Lake, to transport the iron ore and coal of Bradford County. Judge Herrick was delegate to the 1825 Canal Convention at Harrisburg, and a bill passed Legislature providing for a great canal system at a cost of $40,000,000. Commissioners and surveyors began to explore the routes in 1827.

Finale of the Connecticut Controversy at Tioga Point: 1827

The political and economic aspects of the early land feuds, adequately discussed, would fill a volume; the narrative of the legal actions brought by rival claimants, the private quarrels, the recriminations in the press, several more. For Tioga Point was the last storm-center of the Yankee-Pennamite war, the fiercest advocates of 'rights of soil' having moved up to fight out the issue on the border.

It is difficult to subsume the struggle under any modern pair of antonyms—it is able to swallow up a dozen. Neither Puritan versus Quaker, democracy vs. aristocracy, labor vs. capital, liberty vs. tyranny, farmer vs. merchant or any other brace of substantives avail to explain the subtler aspects of the question, the conviction of inherent right and justice possessed by contestants on either side of the argument, each able to justify his position by copious quotation from Scripture.

Apparently numbers of our ancestors crossed the seas because they could brook no interference either in religion, finance, or other personal matters (such as taxation and military conscription). In 1786 they had still to learn that liberty does not grown on a bush, that the reverse of every right is an obligation. *Cooperation* and *compromise* were not yet in the spelling-books.

Viewed in the perspective of history, the relative merits of the two sides

[29] Now Groat property, it still stands on Susquehanna St., retaining many of its quaint 100-year-old features.

of the argument are difficult to assess, nor can all the virtues be ascribed to either side. In many cases the Yankee appears the individualist, intent on personal 'security' in his own narrow domain, 'land for myself and sons.' The Pennamite is more often the socially minded, his imagination swinging out in a wider circle toward the future. The Pennsylvania claimants in our township were foremost in the development of highways, canals and railroads. They were the ones who actually set the Academy going, gave land for churches and cemeteries. They brought in many enterprising business and professional men—the Saltmarshes, Shipmans, Cooks and Willistons. On the Connecticut side, however, we must weigh John Shepard, the Paines and many others—public-spirited, town benefactors if ever there were such, introducing mills, craftsmen, orchards and nurseries, schools, and the first village library. Let us consider the beam balanced.

By 1827, the legal adjustment of many land claims had been effected by the Commonwealth—though not without some heartburnings.[30] The most important issue in our section yet unsettled was that between rival claimants of the Point Farm—the old Indian acreage (there had been no court or legislature to protect the aboriginal owners!). The issue was complicated by local politics (Federalist against Democrat), by the fact that the heirs of both Mathewson and Welles estates were, in the latter years, in legislature—while the youngest Mathewson was about to wed the brother of Samuel McKean, local politician of prominence and U. S. Senator to be. News sheets were born and expired to air the interminable dispute. 'Thistle' and 'Hornet' columnists emerged, epithets were bandied in the *Bradford Settler*, and libel suits instituted. Language sometimes got away from the user—witness 'dry grass whistling through the wind.'

After many delays and false starts, Legislature got under way. Lawyer Townsend Haines reported on Bill 421 (introduced at the instance of Constant Mathewson) exonerating Henry Welles of any unfairness to the heirs of Mathewson, confirming him in possession of the Indian Arrow under Pennsylvania title, but urging the 'moral obligation of government as previously extended to that misguided people, whose credulity was imposed upon by the artifices of the Susquehannah Company.' In view of his *services as a Revolutionary soldier*, and the fact that he was 'the only claimant who had not received the benefit of Legislative acts, it was suggested that Mathewson be accorded compensation, through his heirs, by legislative appropriation. April 14, 1827 a bill authorizing the appraisal of Elisha's acres, the sum to be advanced from the State Treasury, was enacted. Approximately $10,000 was paid the heirs. Lot No. 40 in the village, on which stood the Red Tavern, appears to have been retained also. Here, just south of the Academy, the spacious Mansion House with a large upper hall for public meetings, presently replaced the Old Red Tavern. Henry Welles retained the Farm, on which he had built a grey-stone homestead in 1823, and a number of lots along Main St. standing in his name after a series of adjustments with Caton and Carroll, though he lived only six years to enjoy possession.

For a quarter of a century there was sporadic trouble in the hills, where little Litchfields, Windhams and other offshoots of Connecticut had rooted, and where foreign owners were struggling to understand our laws. But in the Valley the Yankee-Pennamite War was over.

---

[30] Pennsylvania required all on disputed territory to turn in their titles, confirming prior claims, and remunerating those forced to move at as fair a rate as possible per acre.

During this troubled era, a potent agency for peace was the Masonic Order, at whose meetings a momentary peace was effected. The first Masonic rites had been conducted in the valley August 18, 1779 during Sullivan's encampment, at which time an old masonic square was unearthed, calling to mind that a number of Indian chiefs had been admitted to the order, probably at the instance of Sir William Johnson. A local lodge was authorized in 1796, first organized May 21, 1798. Prominent Pennamites and Yankees were members, Satterlee, Welles, the Paines, Dr. Hopkins, Kingsbury, etc. Some of the old insignia and papers of the order are preserved in the Satterlee case in the Museum.

Gallery of Makers of Athens

Sabotage and sniping aside, old border feuds forgotten, let us pass in last review the Makers of Early Athens. Others may recall the tall figure of *John Franklin*, the local Moses, inciting his Wild Yankees at the Red Tavern to rebellion, to the dismay of that other Franklin, old Ben; or rising in Legislature to defy the minions of the city-dwelling, manor-granting Penns. We prefer to picture him as the stalwart husbandman, returning from imprisonment for high treason to take up his allotted acres on the east of Susquehanna; setting down tersely one evening in his diary—our own Israel Putnam—*April 30. Took a fawn from a Wolf. Supposed the Wolfe to be a Dog until too late to kill him.* Or, like Lockwood Smith on his claim west of the rivers, hearing again in old age the martial music of the drum and fifes, and charging imaginary ambushed Indians from tree to tree with Hartley on Browntown Mountain, or with Hand at Chemung or Newtown.

There is the tragic figure, also, of *Colonel Arthur Erwin*, of County Antrim, Ulster, Revolutionary veteran and Pennsylvania owner of a 5000-acre tract on the Chemung (running across Tutelo creek eastward, south of Spanish Hill, north of Lockhart's patent and west of Pickering's). In 1791, on the way to his Bucks County home on the Delaware, after settling his sons on the beautiful flats at Painted Post (the old Indian crossroads where Tioga, Cohocton and Chemung meet), he stopped the night at the home of his tenant and fellowcountryman, Daniel McDuffee.[31] Presumably beyond the range of Wild Yankee depredations, Erwin, with his arm in a sling due to an earlier blow from the pitchfork of a squatter, sat quietly listening to McDuffee's flute—the favorite musical instrument of the pioneer. As McDuffee's wife, who was stitching a seam, stooped to pick up her fallen thimble, a shot over her head killed Erwin. Governor Mifflin offered a $200 reward, his sons added $500 more, but the murderer (probably the squatter who had earlier attacked him) was never apprehended. Such were the early hazards of the border. Col. Franklin took pains to record in his diary his alibi for this evening.

An honored place in our gallery of worthies belongs likewise to the merry little figure of *David Paine*, sprightly gazetteer and columnist, with a hundred schemes in his head for the development of Athens. After a busy and harassed day as secretary of the Susquehannah Company—what with Pennsylvania passing or repealing Confirming, Intrusion or Compromise Acts in the effort to solve the interminable snarl in titles, and Connecticut showing lukewarm in the cause of her stepchild Westmoreland—Bachelor David could rush off gleefully to singing-school in 1800, or lead the dancing with Cloe, Anna, Sally. *Clement Paine* of the classic profile, on the contrary, we prefer to recall in long blue coat on his grey stallion Dick, prancing *capriccioso* down the village street; or on rainy Sundays rapping with his cane on the doors of tardy sleepyheads, summoning all out to divine service.

[31] Whose descendants still live on the original holdings on the Chemung, where they first settled in 1788.

Public benefactor, importer of the stock of 100 different species of fruit-trees from the famous Priestley nurseries at Northumberland, he could nevertheless mount guard relentlessly with shot-gun, when marauding boys skulked along the fence of his favorite apple orchard.

Just before darting down to Charleston to look after Brother Seth's printing business, or taking a year off in Claypoole's office in Philadelphia, Clement could write:

> We have in the place several young ladies and some young gentlemen of very decent polite accomplishments—enough to form a clever party for dancing or other social amusements. And it is remarked by strangers that we have the most genteel collection of young people that can be found for some hundred miles' distance.

Another imperishable tableau has survived the years, of Clement ambling along on Dick with his nose in a book, and almost missing on the highway the cavalcade of his missionary wife and her flock, returning from their labors among the Cherokees in Georgia. Unfortunately, the title of the engrossing volume is lost to history. Was it perchance the *Tempest* (filched from Brother David's village library), or some other play by that incorrigible old Elizabethan pronounced by Clement's wife 'indelicate and worldly?'

Shall we picture *Elizabeth Satterlee Mathewson* as the grim middle-aged widow, mistress of the Red Tavern and mother of six small children, mounting guard with musket and teakettle of boiling water at an upper window, when threatened by the sheriff with a writ of ejection from a Pennsylvania claimant—on Independence Day, 1808? Or shall we recall her as a wide-eyed girl in her teens, steadying a musket on the footboard of the bed of her mother and infant brother, with the turmoil of the battle and massacre of Wyoming all about the cabin?

Another haunting figure in our annals is that of old *Doctor Hopkins*, in dressing-gown and slippers, with white locks awry, rising with the grip of death already on him to burn the unpaid bills of his patients, poor and rich, on the firedogs, under the fine old mantel with fluted columns and classic entablature, where in rufled shirt, wig, knee-buckles and the other accoutrements of fashion he had entertained the aristocracy of France and England.

And how of *Doctor Thomas Huston* of Carlisle, who married Dr. Hopkins' daughter, and whose son was to edit the famous *Athens Gleaner*? He of the 'buttermilk eyes and sandy hair,' tall and lank as a crane, who interspersing Celtic wit with his ministrations, pulled an aching molar for a friend on the steps of the old Exchange, then with a sweeping gesture presented him with both tooth and turnkey. The latter, a fearsome implement, hooked, bone-handled, now reposes on the Museum shelves.

Under the stars, silhouetted against the glowing embers of his gristmill on Cayuta we see another, in a little knot of sweating men in homespun, thanking Providence that quick work has salvaged the wheat-crop of his small colony (which tomorrow must be floated a hundred miles down stream to another miller). Already in imagination he sees the improved structure he will rear on the ruins of the old—bought of Prince Bryant in 1788, when he was a stripling of twenty-three. This is *John Shepard*, patriarch of the upper valley.

Preserved for posterity also is the picture of Dr. Prentice's widow, receiving callers in her Milltown home, under its great spreading elm, with the stuffed peacock in the entry, attired in trained damask gown (looped over her arm), with long slim bodice and elbow sleeves from which droop lace ruffles—mindful of the elegance befitting the daughter of a New England pastor, the friend of a President of Harvard. Mrs. Prentice had survived the terror of Arnold's raid of New London in 1781, salvaging along with the family plate and punch-bowl her famous hand-painted best bed-curtains, scorched fragments of which with their marvelous intricate pattern are preserved today in the Museum.

And whose is the brisk small figure alighting from his horse at the trading-house on the southwest corner of the Square on the Point, darting quick glances over every detail of the scene about him; ordering the repair of a shutter here, a doorknob there; scanning the books and checking the last pelts brought in by the Indian—bear, deer, elk and wolf, marten, mink and otter, panther, beaver and raccoon? Sending out men to bring in the squatters on the land the French refugees wish to buy down the river—though the gay French shops and inns will all but drive him out of business. You have guessed it—this is *Matthias Hollenback,* the Astor of the Upper Susquehanna.

Nor should we forget, among all the dozens of crowding figures '*Commodore*' *Parry,* the genial Welshman at the Chemung toll-gate, whose jests ran up the long village street like wildfire; *Conrad Teeter*, the jovial stage driver, whose stories outwore a hundred years; or the *Wallace brothers,* standing in the snow outside some panelled doorway, to fiddle old Scotch airs at Yuletide.

* * * * * * *

With eighteen hundred and twenty-eight the scene will change, and a new group of actors enter.

Mr Lockharts

Draught

of the Town Lockhartsburgh

On Tyoga